Along the

Texas Forts Trail

Along the
Texas Forts Trail

B. W. Aston
and
Donathan Taylor

Illustrations by Donathan Taylor

University of North Texas Press
Denton, Texas

© 1997 B. W. Aston and Donathan Taylor

5 4 3 2 1

The paper in this book meets the minimum requirements of the
American National Standard for Permanence of Paper for Printed
Library Materials, Z39.48-1984

Permissions
University of North Texas Press
PO Box 311336
Denton, Texas 76203-1336

Library of Congress Cataloging-in-Publication Data

Aston, B. W.
Along the Texas forts trail / by B. W. Aston and Donathan
Taylor ; illustrations by Donathan Taylor.
p.   cm.
Revised edition of : Along Texas old forts trail / Donathan Taylor.
1990
Includes bibliographical references and index.
ISBN 1-57441-035-0 (pbk. : alk. paper)
1. Fortification—Texas—Guidebooks. 2. Historic sites—Texas—
Guidebooks. 3. Automobile travel—Texas—Guidebooks.
4. Trails—Texas—Guidebooks. 5. Texas—Guidebooks.
6. Texas—History, local. I. Taylor, Donathan. II. Richardson,
Rubert Norval, 1891– Along Texas old forts trail. III. Title.
F387.A86 1997
917.6404'63—dc21   97-23491
CIP

Design by Accent Design and Communications

Contents

- Amarillo

- Lubbock

FORT
RICHARDSON

FORT BELKNAP

FORT GRIFFIN

FORT PHANTOM HILL
- Abilene

- Dallas

Ft. Worth

- Tyler

- El Paso
FORT BLISS

FORT CHADBOURNE

FORT CONCHO San Angelo

FORT MASON

FORT
McKAVETT

FORT
STOCKTON

FORT
LANCASTER

- Austin

FORT
DAVIS

Del Rio FORT
CLARK

Presidio FORT
LEATON

Lajitas

FORT
DUNCAN
- Eagle Pass

Piedras
Negras

- Houston

- San Antonio

- Laredo

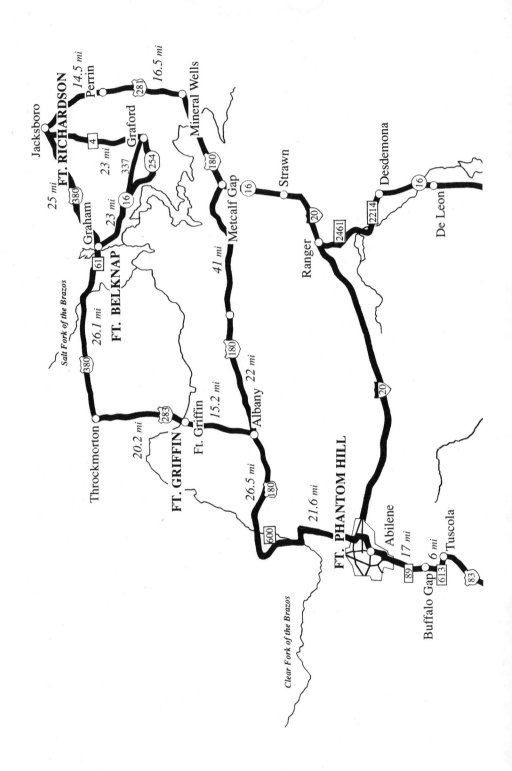

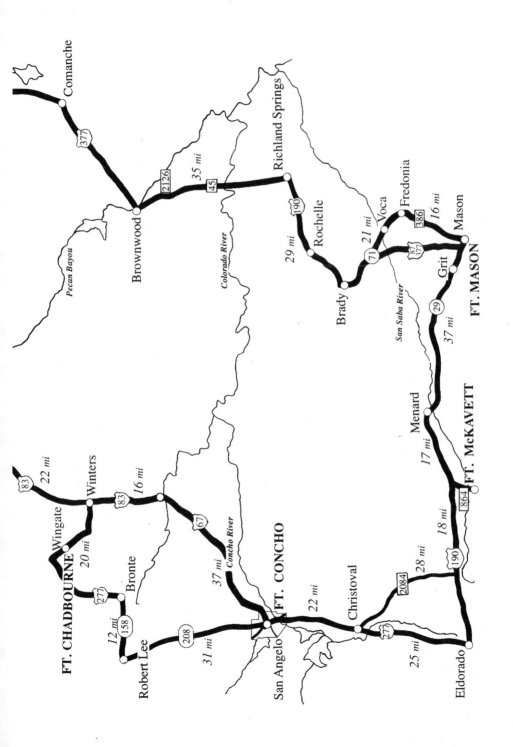

Preface

THE TEXAS FORTS TRAIL had its origin in the mid-1800s when the westward movement of American settlers brought about the need of armed troops and forts to protect them from Indians. On the Texas frontier this rapid advancement called for three lines or cordons to be laid out. Several of these forts in the last two cordons are a part of the Texas Forts Trail, one of ten Texas Travel Trails designated by the Texas Highway Department.

The Texas Travel Trails concept came out of the administration of Governor John Connally who felt that Texas, a land of great contrast, would be more attractive to visitors if they knew what to expect to see in the various areas of the state. Since West Central Texas was especially blessed to have many of the fine forts made famous in Western television series and movies, the state of Texas designated the Forts Trail as one of the travel trails and spent a great deal of time and effort developing and promoting the trails.

Following the Governor's Conference of Tourism in November of 1970, many local communities added their support to the promotion of the Texas Forts Trail. The first such promotional group was developed in Abilene, Texas, in April, 1971, and called itself the Texas Forts Trail Association. This group, led by Richard Dillard, promoted the publication of the first edition of *Along Texas Old Forts Trail* written by the dean of Texas History, Dr. Rupert N. Richardson, illustrated by H. C. Zachry and published by Neil Fry in 1972. It gave the traveler a brief history of the forts and towns along the Trail.

Although much of what Dr. Richardson wrote about the Trail is used in this revision and therefore still very much his work, Donathan Taylor and I have revised the original work with the intent of providing the traveler with additional historical information on the forts and their role in frontier defense, to provide information about the historic sites and historical community programs to allow the traveler to take full advantage of the opportunities offered along the Trail. We have not always chosen the most direct route between Forts, but instead lead the traveler through some of the most scenic terrain of Central Texas. We have also included some of the other forts of Texas that are not located on the Trail. We thought it would be worth your while to drop in on them if you are in the neighborhood.

In this edition of the book, we have updated the tourist information section to make it more reliable for use. The restaurants and overnight accommodations included are beds and breakfasts and independent eating establishments. Major chains and fast-food restaurants are located in almost all of the towns, and are readily available to the traveler. We recommend that your first stop be the chamber of commerce (when available, telephone numbers are provided in the book) or consult the Yellow Pages in the local telephone directories for these locations.

We hope the book helps the traveler enjoy the Forts Trail regardless of where you join or leave it.

B. W. Aston
Hardin-Simmons University

Introduction

THE TASK OF PROVIDING military defense for the Texas Frontier was never an easy one because it was claimed by some of the greatest guerrilla fighters of all times—the Comanches, Kiowas, Apaches, and Lipans. They offered robbery, plunder, torture, and slow death to the settlers at the same time that the land presented them with bountiful game, fertile soil, and grazing land. Protecting a frontier line running from the Red River southwest to El Paso was an impossible task, but following the Mexican War and through the 1850s, the federal government established a line of forts to protect the settlers and travelers across this hostile frontier.

During the Civil War, the frontier forts were virtually abandoned, and the settlers were basically responsible for their own defense. The Indian once again ruled the Texas frontier. Following the war, the government was slow to provide frontier defense, as reconstruction and the protection of the border between Texas and Mexico drew first priority due to the French presence there. When the military did begin to restore old forts and establish new ones, they found the post-war frontier was vastly changed from what it had been during the 1850s. The Indians no longer fought with bows and arrows, but shouldered the latest firearms and had been joined by deserters from the Federal and Confederate Armies. In some cases, they were better armed than either the settlers or the soldiers who fought against them. With their new weapons the Indians were able to inflict tremendous destruction along the Texas frontier line. The years of 1865 and 1866 were recorded as the worst in Texas history, and the frontier receded more than one hundred miles. The settlers bombarded the appointed governor of Texas with their appeals for help, but he simply sent them on to General Philip H. Sheridan, commander of federal forces in Louisiana and Texas. It was not until the summer of 1866 that the frontier defense line began to appear. However, once begun a line of forts rapidly appeared through central Texas from Fort Richardson in the north to Fort Clark in the south and west to Forts Davis and Stockton on the trail to El Paso.

In and around the forts and along the route of Texas Forts Trail, history is abundant and enduring. The old military posts illustrate well the story of the frontier era. With them is linked the memory of the Second Dragoons and tough old Henry H. Sibley who led them. The forts made homes for the Second Cavalry commanded by such officers as Albert Sidney Johnston and Robert E. Lee. In their walls restless Earl Van Dorn planned the campaigns that took him far beyond the boundaries of Texas. Dashing Ranald S. Mackenzie knew them well and grew restive when he had to remain within them too long.

Guardians of a raw young land and focal points of high adventure, the old forts were indispensable in their day of service and it is fitting that they be preserved. Their saga and history will live on.

FORT
Richardson

*The northernmost fort of the line to be established was **Fort Richardson**, located near **Jacksboro** on US Highway 281, 62 miles northwest of Fort Worth.*

Jacksboro and Jack County were named after two Texas Revolutionary patriots, brothers William H. and Patrick C. Jack. The brothers were from a family of patriots. Their grandfather, Captain James Jack of Mecklenburg, North Carolina, was one of the signers of the famous Mecklenburg Declaration of Independence during the American Revolution. Their father, Patrick Jack, a prominent lawyer in Wilkes County, Georgia, was an officer in the War of 1812. The Jack brothers both graduated from the University of Georgia with law degrees, and shortly afterward headed for Texas. William arrived in San Felipe in 1830, and was joined by Patrick in 1832. Patrick was arrested with Will-

1

iam B. Travis at Anahuac in 1832; William was with Sam Houston at San Jacinto.

After the war, Patrick served in the Texas House and as District Judge of the Sixth District. William served as Secretary of State under Burnet in 1836, and served terms in both the Texas House and Senate. The brothers died of yellow fever in 1844.

The Jacksboro community began in 1853 in the neighborhood of Lost Creek during the perilous Indian era. The name was changed to Mesquiteville and later to Jacksboro. Today Jacksboro is a community of approximately four thousand inhabitants who are very much aware of their historical background and the importance their city played on the frontier. On the square is the Fort Richardson Hotel that served as post headquarters for Major and Brevet Colonel S. H. (Paddy) Starr from July 4, 1866, to April 1867. Just west of downtown is the Jack County Museum, located in possibly the oldest house in Jack County, and the site of the birth of the "Corn Club" which became the 4-H Club in 1907. Just a few blocks south of the square is Fort Richardson State Park. Jacksboro holds a series of events throughout the year to profile their community and its history.

The greatest event in the history of early-day Jacksboro was the arrival in September 1858 of stage coaches carrying mail and passengers from Saint Louis and San Francisco. These semi-weekly coaches of the Butterfield (or Southern) Overland Mail Company continued to run until the opening of the Civil War. They provided the north Texas frontier with direct and rapid communication. Jacksboro truly was "on the main line."

After the Civil War the country around Jacksboro was flailed by marauding Indians. The "Great White Father" in Washington proposed to place the Indians on the reservations and maintain them there. The vicinity that was selected as homes for the Comanches, Kiowas, and Plains Apaches was just north of the Red River, less than a hundred miles away. Here the Indians were taught to farm and to live like white people. But these Indians did not want to live like white people, and they boasted that they had never planted seed of any kind. The old men signed treaties agreeing to be good Indians, but the young men continued to visit the frontier of north Texas (the country they still claimed as their own) to steal horses, take women and children captive, and lift an occasional scalp. Jacksboro and its vicinity needed protection.

In July of 1866, Captain G. C. Cram with Company I—consisting of twenty-nine men and thirty-nine horses—arrived, pitched their tents, and established the Post of Jacksboro. During the next few months Companies A, D, E, F, K, and L arrived along with Major Samuel H. Starr. That brought the post strength to 465 officers and men and 325 horses.

The troops were housed in tents and picket-style log houses. The post was without any of the basic necessities, which left many of the men in rags and nearly barefoot. Consequently, the men spent much of their time evading their duties—playing cards, and drinking Pine-Tope or White Mule whiskey. By December 30 eight men had deserted. Because of lack of interest and the poor quality of mounts available to field a detail, only two deserters were caught and returned. (Hamilton 1988, 18–19) With similar results Lieutenant William A. Rafferty and Company I were sent in pursuit of the Indians who had killed post hay cutters Ernest Jones, his son, and two blacks. Rafferty trailed the Indians to the Little Wichita River and returned without ever encountering them.

Hospital and
morgue.

Other Indian raids in Wise County that left one woman dead and
two children and several horses taken captive also went unpun-
ished. (Hamilton 1988)

By March 1867, the military decided to abandon Fort Jacksboro.
Companies A and E were ordered to a site in Clay County, about
twenty-five miles north, called Buffalo Springs. It was closer to the
Red River and was believed to possess greater quantities of wood
and water. The rest of the command under Major Starr reformed
in Fort Belknap. (Hamilton 1988, 21)

The military's experiences at Buffalo Springs proved to be quite
hectic. Although closer to the Indians, Buffalo Springs was further from the base of supply in Austin. In comparison its sparse
life made Jacksboro look good to the men. Even so, the military
planned to make it a permanent post, and by the summer of 1867
some one-hundred civilian workers had begun construction of
the post.

All activity came to a halt on July 19, when some three hundred Indians hit a timber detail, killing a teamster and carrying
off twenty-four mules. Two days later survivors arrived at
Richardson with news of the attack. Benjamin Hutchins and thirty
mounted men were sent in pursuit, leaving behind forty-five soldiers, sixty civilians, and twenty-seven rifles. Late that day the Indians hit Buffalo Springs and might have overwhelmed it, had they

not been scared off by the shouting and clatter of an approaching mounted column. In reality this was the sixty civilian employees running from their camp, about half a mile to the north, for the protection of the fort. Their arrival confused the Indians into calling off their attack and camping nearby to determine their future course of action. They withdrew altogether two days later when Captain Hutchins and his detail returned.

An extended drought added to the problems of Buffalo Springs during the summer of 1867 and placed the future of the site in jeopardy. This became especially true when a spring of good water was discovered near Jacksboro. An inspection board condemned Buffalo Springs on November 18, 1867. (Hamilton 1988, 22–25) The following day Captain Daniel Madden of Company E, Sixth United States Cavalry, received orders to return to Jacksboro and establish Fort Richardson.

When Captain Madden arrived in Jacksboro he found that the previously constructed buildings had been torn down and the materials used by the local populace. It was therefore necessary to begin all over. A new site was chosen on a high rolling prairie about half a mile to the southwest of Jacksboro, on the south side of Lost Creek, a tributary of the Trinity.

Fort Richardson was named for General Israel Bush "Fighting Dick" Richard, who died of wounds received at the Battle of Antietam in 1862. Estimated cost of the fort ranged as high as $800,000, but unfortunately the plans laid out by the government were not followed. Instead the picket style barracks built for the troops were poor and inadequate, and the post hospital, bakery, guard house, and magazine were built of native limestone.

Fort Richardson's location, only seventy miles from the Indian territory, placed it in a strategic position to protect the local settlers from continued Indian depredations, to launch campaigns against the marauding Indians, to protect the flow of travelers across the region, and to keep the cattle trails open from Texas to

Kansas. The construction of the fort brought a boom period to Jacksboro, and a higher desertion rate at the post. The men felt that they had joined the army to fight Indians not to work as common laborers in the stone quarry or on the wood detail.

Although the fort was charged with the protection of the settlers of the area, its record during the early days was less than satisfactory. As a matter of fact, the Indians continued to raid the area at will with little fear of the soldiers. This situation had developed because of the Quaker Peace Policy implemented by President U. S. Grant in 1869.

According to the people in the northeast who had developed the policy, the Indian problem did not need military force to solve it. Kindness, religious instruction and agricultural training would do the job. It was the Quakers who were first chosen to initiate the new policy, which made the reservations a sanctuary on which the military had no authority. The Indians could leave the reservation, raid the white settlements south of the Red River, and then flee back to the reservation where they could not be touched. (Richardson and Rister, 307–08) This situation began to change following the battle at the Little Wichita River in July of 1870, between Captain Curwin B. McClellan with fifty-six men and Kicking Bird's war party of some one-hundred warriors, among whom were Stumbling Bear, Lone Wolf, and Satank. Kicking Bird had been goaded into the raid by Lone Wolf and Satank.

On July 5, the Kiowa war party entered Texas with orders for the braves not to go on individual forays; however some did, and robbed a mail stage at Rock Station on Salt Creek Prairie about sixteen miles from Fort Richardson. The command at Fort Richardson, smarting from an earlier defeat, ordered Captain McClellan to "pursue and severely chastise the Indians." On the morning of the twelfth, McClellan caught up with what he thought was Kicking Bird's major force all dressed up in their finery. McClellan moved forward about five hundred yards and prepared to engage the enemy, only to find himself flanked by an equal number of hostiles. From that point on, McClellan's primary concern was to fight an orderly retreat that kept his command intact and alive. The battle had begun at 10:00 A.M., and did not break off until nightfall when Kicking Bird felt his honor had been restored.

Some of his braves picked up the action the next morning. McClellan, thinking that the full force was after him, destroyed the supplies that were not immediately transportable and again began an orderly retreat to Fort Richardson with only two men killed and twelve wounded. However, the braves chose not to continue their advance. The result was that Kicking Bird regained some of his prestige as a leader, and McClellan restored some prestige to the fighting ability of the men at Fort Richardson. Thirteen of McClellan's men were awarded the Medal of Honor, and he was praised for his actions. Kicking Bird later spoke of McClellan's orderly retreat and of the number of Indians that lost their lives during the engagement. (Hamilton 1988, 54–60)

The battle at the Little Wichita River and other encounters on the Salt Creek Prairie between Fort Belknap and Fort Richardson during the fall and spring of 1870 and 1871, signaled the need for a change. On March 20, 1871, Colonel James Oakes and the Sixth

Officers' quarters.

Cavalry were transferred to Fort Harker, Kansas. Colonel Oakes's replacement was Colonel Ranald Slidell Mackenzie and the Fourth Cavalry that arrived on April 8. Mackenzie was not at all pleased with the condition of the fort. He was particularly displeased when the ladies of the Fourth had to place their sleeping gear in flea-infested huts, and his men had to pitch their tents along the banks of Lost Creek.

The Indians were quick to challenge the new command. On April 19, they killed John W. Weburn on the Salt Creek Prairie, and led raids near the fort for the next two days. Mackenzie sent two details in pursuit of the attackers. Although the troopers did not encounter Indians, they did spend nine days in the field and covered several hundred miles, a unique change in action for the troopers of Fort Richardson. (Hamilton 1988, 65–68)

The major event that altered the future of Fort Richardson involved William Tecumseh Sherman, senior military officer of the United States. Sherman was in Texas for an inspection of the post to see for himself if things were as bad as they were being reported. With him was Randolph Barnes Marcy, Inspector General of the Army, who had known the Texas frontier for nearly twenty years. Sherman arrived at Fort Richardson on May 17, not knowing how close he and his party had come to probable annihilation. Two days earlier Satank along with Satanta, Addoetta, Maman-ti the Owl Prophet, and over one hundred Kiowa, Comanche, Kiowa-Apache, Arapaho, and Cheyenne warriors had left the reservation for a big raid into Texas. Satank and his followers were encamped on the Salt Creek Prairie and had watched Sherman and his party pass. They had been allowed to do so only because Maman-ti's magic had warned Satank that there would be two white parties on the trail, and the second to pass would be the easier prey. (Hamilton 1988, 71, 78)

News of what could have happened to Sherman arrived the next day when a wounded teamster of the Warren Wagon Train arrived to tell of the attack. The wagon master and six teamsters were killed while the other five managed to escape the massacre on Salt Creek Prairie.

Sherman immediately ordered Mackenzie, with four companies of the Fourth and two companies from Fort Griffin, into all-out pursuit of the raiders. Mackenzie arrived at the scene of the massacre on the nineteenth. The surgeon made the following report to Sherman:

> I examined on May 19, 1871, the bodies of five citizens killed near Salt Creek by Indians on the previous day. All the bodies were addled with bullets, covered with gashes and the skulls crushed . . . with an axe. . . . Some of the bodies exhibited signs of having been stabbed with arrows, one of the bodies . . . [was] found fastened with a chain to the pole of a wagon lying over a fire with the face to the ground, the tongue being cut out. (Hamilton 1988, 82–83)

Mackenzie buried the bodies and turned toward the Red River in pursuit. Rain had wiped out the raiders' tracks and by the 21st the Indians were all back on the reservation. Finding out who was responsible for the raid was not hard as Satanta boasted of his exploit and said that any other chief who laid claim to the honor was a liar. Texans had been known to shoot Indians on sight and now Satanta was elated at the thought that he had partially evened the score. The Indians could not be arrested on the reservation, so through Lawrie Tatum, the Quaker Agent in charge of the Comanches, Kiowas, and Prairie Apache Reservation, the military managed to get the Indians to meet with Sherman at Fort Sill to discuss their grievances. On May 27, when they arrived, Sherman had Satanta, Big Tree and Satank arrested. Some tense moments followed, but outright conflict was avoided by Satanta's intervention.

The three leaders were jailed to await the arrival of Mackenzie to escort them back to Fort Richardson. Sherman left Fort Sill on May 30 to continue his inspection. Mackenzie finally arrived at Fort Sill on June 4, after a fruitless search for the Indian marauders in the western Indian territory. He was surprised to find the culprits in jail. He left for Fort Richardson on June 8. Along the way Satank, who had vowed that he would rather die than face trial, managed to free himself from his handcuffs and attack the guards, provoking gunfire that brought his immediate death.

The arrival of Mackenzie and his prisoners at Fort Richardson on June 15 created a festive occasion, and put in motion one of the most famous trials to be carried out in Jacksboro. On July 5 and 6, Big Tree and Satanta were found guilty of murder and condemned to hang. However, Governor Edmund J. Davis first commuted them to life imprisonment, and then in 1873 paroled both chiefs. Shortly thereafter they violated their paroles by leading new raids into Texas. Satanta was taken in 1874 and placed in the prison at Huntsville where he died after a fall from an upper story window of the hospital. Big Tree was arrested the following year, but was later released upon the request of federal officials. He died in 1929 at Anadarko, Oklahoma. (Hamilton 1988, 89–96)

Meanwhile Colonel Mackenzie, who commanded Fort Richardson from April 1871 to December 1872, was gathering troops from all over Texas in preparation for launching a major foray from Fort Richardson against the plains Indians. Mackenzie's first expedition, August 4 to September 13, was more or less a shake-down exercise to gain additional field experience. However the second, September 24 to November 18, took him 509 miles where he encountered both hostiles and severe winter weather. Neither campaign had decisive encounters, although Mackenzie had been wounded during a battle in Blanco Canyon.

Mackenzie's third campaign began on June 19, 1872, when he left Fort Richardson to join forces from Forts Griffin and Concho, and mounted the first major campaign against the Indians on the Llano Estacado (the "Staked Plain," which refers to the High Plains of Northwest Texas that extend west to the Pecos River, south to the Edwards Plateau area, east along a line to include parts of Dawson, Borden, Gara, Crosby, Dickens, Motley, Floyd, Brisco and Armstrong counties). The plains are broken by rugged canyons created by stream erosion of which some of the better known ones are Yellow House Canyon, near Lubbock, Blanco Canyon in Crosby and Floyd County, and Palo Duro Canyon south of Amarillo.

By August 7 Mackenzie was within twenty miles of Fort Sumner, New Mexico, where he resupplied his forces and then moved on to Fort Bascum before turning back east via Palo Duro Canyon in search of Comanches and Comancheros. Finally on September 28, Mackenzie encountered the camp of Kotsoteka Comanche Chief Mow-way in a valley on the south side of the north fork of the Red River. Mackenzie and his troops enjoyed their first major victory taking 130 women and children prisoner, capturing 175 large and 87 small teepees, and a horse herd that ranged in size from 800 to 3,000, depending upon which account you read.

Mackenzie burned the village, making sure that nothing of value was left for Indian use, and then encamped about two miles distant. During the next two nights, the Comanches raided the captured horse herd, leaving Mackenzie with only fifty ponies and nine mules, and somewhat embarrassed. The captives were sent to Fort Concho while Mackenzie returned to Fort Richardson on October 23, 1872. The experience gained from that expedition convinced Mackenzie that he needed to be closer to the theater of operation. In March 1873, Mackenzie moved his headquarters to Fort Concho, and Fort Richardson began its decline. (Hamilton 1988, 129–35)

Fort Richardson's final participation in the Indian campaigns began in August of 1874 and lasted for seven months, when the Quaker Peace Policy was removed and the military was ordered to pursue the marauding Indians wherever the trail led. The army finally had the opportunity to launch total war against the Indians. When the great Red River War ended, the Indian threat to Texas was over, ending the need for Fort Richardson. (Hamilton 1988, 152–60) By May 23, 1878, the command and the properties of Fort Richardson had been transferred to Forts Griffin and Concho. (Whisenhunt 1963, 26)

In 1963 the National Parks Service designated Fort Richardson a Registered National Historic Landmark and restoration of the fort began. Today there is an interpretive center that gives the visitor a quick overview of the fort and its role on the frontier. Also the hospital, officers quarters, and several men's barracks are restored. Alongside the fort is Fort Richardson State Park that provides campsites and wilderness trails for the traveler.

With the departure of the troops, Jacksboro settled down to being a normal town. The presence of the military had been a boon to the economy of Jacksboro. There were all types of jobs to be had and money to be made. Of course it attracted all types of individuals, and along the north bank of Lost Creek numerous shanties appeared, most in the form of saloons. At one time twenty-seven of these were in operation within the city limits. It was said that the Wichita Saloon had taken in as much as $1,000 a night on several occasions, leaving drunk soldiers lining the route from the square to the post.

Thousands of drifters passed through Jacksboro to add their particular flair to the city, and it is reported that even Lottie Deno of Fort Griffin fame got her start in Jacksboro. In Mrs. Huckabay's book, Miss Lottie shows up in Jacksboro in 1870 where she seems to have led a more boisterous life. "From 1871 to 1875 she paid an occupation tax as a retail liquor dealer and more than once paid fines for maintaining a disorderly house." (Huckabay, 154–55) The presence of Buffalo Soldiers—black soldiers so called by the Indians because their hair reminded them of buffalo hair—at the post also led to confrontations with the white settlers from time to time. But that all came to an end as the military moved west.

TOURIST INFORMATION

(When possible please call ahead to be sure these services are still available.)

Fort Richardson State Historical Park

Points of Interest:	A reconstructed officers' barracks serves as Interpretive Center, which is open daily. Six of the original stone buildings exist: morgue, bakery, magazine, commissary, hospital, and part of the guardhouse.
Activities:	Camping with electricity, picnic sites, rest rooms, shower; hiking trails; pond, fishing
Annual events:	(940-567-3506) April: Annual Meeting of Friends of Fort Richardson May: Frontier Festival August: Hoof-N-Hair Cookoff November: Military Re-Enactment December: Christmas in the park

Jacksboro (940/567-2602)

Population:	3,407
Lakes:	Lake Jacksboro, Lost Creek Reservoir
Points of interest:	**Jack County Museum**, located in the oldest house in Jack County, two rooms furnished with period furnishing depicting home life; one room dedicated to Jack County veterans; memorabilia on Tom M.

Marks who organized the club which later became the 4 H Club.

Restored 100 year old log cabin, furnished with period furniture, 257 West Belknap, just west of the square

Nineteenth-century buildings around the courthouse

Annual events:
January: Jack County Youth Fair & Livestock Show
March: Rattlesnake Safari
June: Jack County Sheriff's Posse Rodeo & Parade
July: Twin Lakes Summerfest
December: Christmas Parade.

Accommodations:
Fort Richardson Motel, Highway 281
Butterfield Depot Motel, 544 North Main, 940-567-5567
Jacksboro Country Inn Bed & Breakfast, 940-567-6600
Jacksboro Inn, Highway 281, 940-567-3751
R.V. Parks:
Fort Richardson State Historical Park
Mitchell's R.V. Park, Farm Market Road 2210 East Perrin, 940-798-4615

Restaurants:
Angora Roadhouse, 103 Sewell, 940-567-3575
City Drug Store, 104 E. Belknap , 940-567-5576
Chicken Express, 715 N. Main, 940-567-2625
Country Cousins' Cafe, 108 N. Church, 940-567-2287
Dairyland Drive-Inn, 323 S. Main, 940-567-5000 or 940-567-3705
Dairy Queen, Hwy. 281 North, 940-567-5362
The Deli, 400-A S. Main, 940-567-2442

Green Frog Restaurant, 416 N. Main, 940-567-3724

Herd Hamburgers, 401 N. Main

The Korner Donut Shop, 125 E. College, 567-6051

Pizza Pro, 120 E. Belknap, 940-567-6511 or 567-5542

The Village Kitchen, Highway 281 South, 940-567-5902

The Feed Store, 508 S. Main, 940-567-3331

Specialty Shopping:

Bill's Dollar Store, 503 N. Main, 940-567-3350

City Drug Store, 104 E. Belknap, 940-567-5576

Diamond Supermarket, 201 E. South St., 940-567-2212

The Gallery, 114 E. Belknap, 940-567-2676

Gibson Pharmacy, 711 N. Main, 940-567-3716

E. B. Mott Co., 103 E. Archer, 940-567-5651

Now & Then Shop, 105 E. Archer, 940-567-5095

TEXAS FORTS TRAIL

FORT

Belknap

*Southward from Jacksboro take Highway 4 to **Graford**, which takes its name from its position halfway between Graham and Weatherford.*

The first settler of the community was George R. Bevers in 1854, who located at Flat Rock Crossing on Big Keechi Creek, three miles east. This became a well-known stopping place on the road between Weatherford and Fort Belknap. Today there is not much in Graford although it is the home of Big Tex porkskins. Other than for the scenic drive, you might want to bypass Graford and go straight to Graham from Jacksboro along Highway 380.

*From Graford take either Highway 337, the more direct route to **Graham**, or Highway 16 which stays on the Forts Trail along the west side of Possum Kingdom.*

Graham was founded in 1872 by Gustavus and Edwin S. Graham, and it soon became a mercantile and milling center. The Cattle Raisers Association of Texas, which was the predecessor of the Texas and Southwestern Cattle Raisers Association, was organized here in 1877.

Within the limits of Graham, a short distance south of Court House Square, is an official state historical marker which rests on the line of the old Brazos Indian Reservation that had been established in February 1854 by the Texas legislature. Major Robert S. Neighbors, supervising Indian agent, and Captain Randolph B. Marcy surveyed the eight-square league tract located on both sides of the Brazos River in Young County. From 1855 to 1859, Indians of various tribes including Anadarko, Caddo, Tehuacana, Tonkawa, Waco, and some Cherokees, Choctaws, Delawares, Shawnees, and others were placed on the reservation. At one point there were over one thousand Indians on the Brazos River Reservation who were making great progress in adapting to the white man's ways in agriculture, stock-raising, and other acts considered civil. In contrast, activities of marauding non-reservation Indians provoked so much hostility along the frontier that it was necessary to move them near Anadarko in the Indian Territory.

Fort Belknap is a short distance west of Graham on Highway 61.

In frontier times "all trails led to Fort Belknap." During the 1850s, it was a dividing place, separating the frontier settlements from the unguarded frontier. Even though violence by marauding Indians was not uncommon east of the fort, there was a modicum of security there. West of Fort Belknap, anything might happen to the traveler or to any person bold enough to live there. The Butterfield Overland Mail people, whose horses were at first a rich windfall for the Comanches, learned that at Fort Belknap they had better change to mules. Chief Isakeep told Captain Marcy that his four sons were a great comfort to him in his old age, since they could steal more horses than any other four young men in the tribe. However, a self-respecting Comanche would not ride a mule and was not likely to steal one.

The site for Fort Belknap, overlooking the Salt Fork of the Brazos River about ten miles north of the confluence of the Clear Fork and an equal distance from Marcy's Trail, was selected by Brevet Brigadier General William Goldsmith Belknap on June 24, 1851. He was joined by Captain Marcy, and together they moved west to locate two additional posts to provide protection on the route west. The problem of constructing the fort was placed in the hands of its first commanding officer, Captain Carter L. Stevenson, Fifth Infantry. After sinking two deep dry wells and suffering a summer drought, Captain Stevenson abandoned the chosen site on November 1, 1851, for a location, about two miles south. There, springs near the bank of the Brazos furnished water for the fort until a well was sunk in 1857.

Fort Belknap soon became a hub of connecting roads stretching south to Fort Worth, Dallas, and San Antonio; west to Camp Cooper, Forts Phantom Hill and Chadbourne; and to the Indian agencies in Young and Throckmorton Counties. Beginning in the fall of 1858, the Butterfield Overland Mail Company used Fort Belknap as a depot where mules were kept to pull the stage through Indian territory. About half a mile east of the fort, the little village of Fort Belknap was laid out and became the county seat of Young County on its organization in 1856. The future of the town was on shaky ground when Fort Belknap was abandoned prior to the Civil

War and when a fire in the summer of 1860 destroyed most of its businesses. Both events led to the slow dissolution of county government that by 1865 caused the state to move the county records to Jacksboro. When the county was reorganized in 1874, Graham was selected as the county seat. The village of Fort Belknap continued to survive until the twentieth century.

In December of 1855, the famed Second United States Cavalry arrived at Fort Belknap. The regiment of 750 men and 800 horses had marched from Jefferson Barracks, Missouri. Mrs. Eliza Johnston, wife of Albert Sidney Johnston, the Texan colonel in command, told the story of the march in her diary. "A thousand camp fires blazing around the white tents . . . soldiers standing around . . . cooking their supper . . . talking over expected pleasures of the campaign." At four o'clock in the morning, trumpets sounded "boots and saddles," and at six all started merrily.

As the regiment approached Fort Belknap at the Christmas season it was caught in a severe blizzard. Wives of officers at the post generously invited Mrs. Johnston to bring her little children

Powder magazine.

in and share their relatively comfortable quarters. But the brave woman declined their invitations. Since there was not room in the officers quarters for all the women and children with the regiment it seemed fitting and in accord with the high morale of the organization that the colonel's lady and children continue to get along in a tent, shivering around a little fire in the center.

The Second Cavalry moved on to other posts at the time but later contingents served at Fort Belknap, notably Companies D and F, commanded by Major George H. Thomas who would one day win the accolade, the Rock of Chickamauga. Fort Belknap was a sort of hinge for the north Texas frontier, and its forces were involved in some way or other in most of the important military efforts of the 1850s. For instance, in 1858 Major Earl Van Dorn marched away from here to fight the Comanches north of the Red River and not all of his force returned. Lieutenant Cornelius Van Camp, a sergeant, and three privates were killed at Rush Springs, Indian Territory on October 1.

The military could not have picked a worse time to pull out of the region. On February 17 through 23, 1859, the last of the troops left Fort Belknap for Camp Cooper. During the fall of 1858, white renegades had raided the Brazos Indian Reservation, killing seven Caddo and Anadarko Indians, while red renegades raided several settlements in the region. Add to this confusion the murder of Robert Neighbors, supervising agent for Texas Indians, on the streets of Fort Belknap. Neighbors was shot and killed by Edward Cornett apparently because of his remarks condemning the recent slaying of Indians by white men. It did not seem to be a time for abandoning the fort. Major Thomas, however, was quite pleased to leave the area, as the whiskey peddlers of Belknap caused him a great deal of discipline problems.

For a brief period in 1867 it looked as if Fort Belknap would once again be a link in the defenses of the Texas frontier. Lieuten-

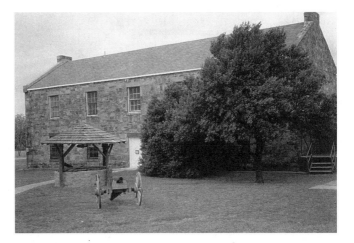

Commissary
stone museum.

ant Colonel Samuel D. Sturgis was not at all pleased with his as-
signment when he was ordered to reestablish the post, and he
immediately began a campaign to get the post closed. Sturgis centered his argument on the lack of availability of adequate drinking water. In one report he stated that a test of a quart of river
water evaporation yielded a tablespoonful of salt. From another
source comes the information that unknown to the officer this
particular quart of water had been loaded with extra salt. Later he
reported that the fort was untenable. He wrote:

> The camp and old buildings are located on a clear and
> level patch of sand and are surrounded on three sides
> (within easy pistol range) by a dense growth of small tim-
> ber and underbrush which would serve the Indians admi-
> rably for cover, in case they determined to venture an attack
> upon the place. . . . (Richardson 1963, 276)

Just in case some officer suggested that he clear the area, he
pointed out that his 112 men could not do the job in a year of
hacking. To further his argument, he reported that there were
four or five thousand Indians in the vicinity near Fort Cobb, five

or six day's march from Belknap, that could effectively cut off his water supply.

In spite of all his complaints it seemed that the military was going to locate a permanent post at Belknap. Sturgis sent Lieutenant H. B. Mellen to locate a better site. One was found about thirty-five miles southwest on the Clear Fork of the Brazos in northeast Shackelford County. The site became Fort Griffin, and Belknap was finally abandoned in the fall of 1867. The remains of the fort were once again taken over by the civilians of Belknap, and over the years the stones of the fort were carted off until only the magazine and part of the corn house are standing. (Richardson 1963, 274–76)

The present-day excellent restoration of Fort Belknap was made possible by Senator Ben G. Oneal in 1935, as part of the Texas Centennial project. Restored buildings include the magazine, corn house, commissary store, two infantry quarters, the well, and a kitchen. The fort contains a fine museum of tools, weapons, and furnishings used on the Texas frontier. The corn house contains a museum of ladies' apparel, many of which were worn by the first ladies of Texas and gowns of Mrs. Dwight D. Eisenhower, Mrs. Douglas MacArthur, and Lady Bird Johnson. The post also contains the Fort Belknap Archives, which concentrates on materials relating to the fort, but also contains Texana materials. The fort can be used for conferences, and is the site of the annual meeting of the Fort Belknap Historical Association. Finally, the Cox Grape Arbor provides a fine place for a picnic on a lazy summer day.

TOURIST INFORMATION

(When possible please call ahead to be sure these services are still available.)

Fort Belknap (940-846-3222)

Registered National Historic Landmark. Fort Belknap is owned by the citizens of Young County and no charge is made for its use. Guided tours of the Museums may be arranged by writing or calling: Fort Belknap, Newcastle, TX 76372 (940-846-3222)

Points of interest:

The Commissary contains a museum and gift shop, open from 9–5 every weekday except Wednesday. On Sunday it is open from 1:30–5. The museum contains tools, weapons and furniture used on the frontier. Pictures of former officers stationed at the fort are of special interest.

The sound of "Reveille" and "Taps," the voices of soldiers and the sound of horses' hoofs echo across the **Parade Grounds of old Fort Belknap**.

Cox Grape Arbor, where many family reunions and other gatherings are held each year, was planted by Burl W. Cox, an early day Belknap school teacher, farmer and naturalist. Some of the Mustang Grape vines covering this arbor are nine feet tall and measure fifty-four inches in circumference.

Powder Magazine is one of the best preserved of the original structures.

Infantry Barracks #1 has been converted into an auditorium and **Barracks #2** is now a dining hall.

The Archives Building is located in Barracks #4 and is open on Saturdays from 8:30–5:30. It contains much Texas history and rare documents. The Archives are also the depository of the Fort Belknap Genealogical Society Association.

Corn House, now known as the Womans' Building, contains mostly ladies' apparel, many of the pieces being gowns of the first ladies of Texas, of Mamie Eisenhower, Mrs. Douglas MacArthur and Lady Bird Johnson.

Fort Belknap Cemetery is located 1/2 mile east of the Fort. Major R. S. Neighbors, who was murdered on the streets of Belknap, is buried there; one lone Union soldier, Miles Cook, several confederate soldiers and S. P. Johnson, frontier Ranger and Indian fighter are buried there.

Annual Events: July: Fourth at the Fort is celebrated annually with food booths, arts & crafts and an evening fireworks display

Graham (800-256-4844, 940-549-3355)

Chamber of Commerce, American Legion Building, P.O. Box 299, Graham, TX 76450

Population: 9,014

Lakes: Graham and Possum Kingdom

Points of interest: **Courthouse Square** is recognized as the largest courthouse square in the United States, measuirng 620 feet by 890 feet. The Cattle Raisers Association of Texas was formed under a large live oak tree near the northwest corner of the square.

Old Courthouse Archway

Graham Art Museum, on Courthouse Square, in the Old Post Office Building

Robert E. Richeson Confederate Air Force Cactus Squadron Memorial Museum. The West Texas Wing of the Confederate Airforce has restored a SB2-C

"Helldiver" aircraft to its World War II flying condition, the only aircraft of its kind in flying condition. Known during WWII as "The Beast," for its ungainly flying characteristics, the SB2-C is a medium bomber designed to fly off aircraft carriers. The museum also contains WWII memorabilia, including munitions, uniforms, items of everyday military life, and a large collection of model aircraft of the era. Open Thursdays from 1–5. Other times can be arranged by calling the Graham Chamber of Commerce. Located at the Graham Municipal Airport, at the intersection of Hwy 380 By-pass and Jacksboro Hwy.

The Library of Graham, located in Shawnee Springs Park (see below)

Rock Island Railroad Station

Belknap Civilian Cemetery, located in a field 1/2 mile east of Fort Belknap off SH #61. Caution: Cars can get stuck in the sand.

Shawnee Springs Park once was home to the Brazos River Indian Reservation. The park, located at the south end of Graham on both sides of State Highway 16, contains a children's area, picnic tables and on the northeast side of the park, the Library of Graham. A nature trail is the location of the original Shawnee spring—a four foot deep sandstone formation used by the Indians of the Brazos Indian Reservation.

Annual Events:

March: Rotary Club's Possum Pedal 100 Daffodil Days

April: Confederate Air Force Fly-in, Spring Stroll, Tour, and Parade

May: Annual Lake Country Art Festival

July: Fourth at the Fort—Fort Belknap

September: Wild West Possum Fest & Backyard BBQ & Chili Cook-Off

November: Christmas Store

December: Starlight Extravaganza Stroll & Christmas Parade

Accommodations:

The Cliffs, Possum Kingdom Lake, 940-779-4021, 800-621-8534

Gate Way Inn, 1401 Hwy 16 S, 940-549-0222

Rodeway Inn, 1919 Hwy 16 S, 940-549-8320

Ponderosa RV & Mobil Home Park, 2400 Hwy 16 S, 940-549-3708

Travelers Inn and Restaurant, 1516 Hwy 16 S, 940-549-0274

Victorian Memories Bed and Breakfast, Cherry Street, 940-549-4005

Camps on east side of Possum Kingdom:

Rock Creek Camp, 940-779-2766

Willow Beach RV Park and Marine, Hwy 2353 to Willow Beach Road, 940-779-3004

Rainbow RV Park, 111 Hwy 2353, 940-779-2933

Sky Camp Resort and RV Park, Hwy 2353, 940-779-2741

Camp Constantin (Boy Scouts), 940-779-2131

Camp Grady Spruce (Frontier Camp), 940-779-9202

One Mountain Place, FM 2951, 1/4 mile west off Possum Kingdom Road 36, 940-799-2333

Scenic Point Marina and Lodge, Possum Kingdom, 940-799-2366

Sandbar Village, FM 2951, 940-779-2922

P. K. Lodge, Graford, 940-779-2757

Camps on west side of Possum Kingdom:

Possum Kingdom State Park, 940-549-1803

Bailey's on Possum Kingdom, 940-549-1871

Fox Hollow Camp, Graham, 940-549-1801

Possum Hollow RV Park and Cabins, 940-549-1873

Lakeshore Marina and RV Park, 5501 Lakeshore
Drive, 940-549-2518

Bass Hollow Camp, 940-549-0104

Restaurants:

Carmen's Kitchen, 1210 Fourth Street, 940-549-3474

Casteel's Seafood & Steak, 400 Elm Street, 940-549-
5320

Chicken Express, 1322 Hwy 16 S, 940-549-2200

China Inn, 1602 Hwy 16 S, 940-549-8442

Dairy King, 910 Elm Street, 940-549-3718

Dairy Queen (Airport), Hwy 380 Bypass, 940-549-
2500; (Southside), 1310 Hwy 16 S, 940-549-4977

El Gallo, 608 Oak Street, (west side of Square) 940-
549-8838

Flo's Burgers, 610 Oak Street, 940-549-3474

Gateway Supper club, 1401 Hwy 16 S, 940-549-6603

Golden China, 1104 Cypress, 940-549-6001

Golden Fried Chicken, 1445 East Fourth Street, 940-
549-8650

Jim & Sylvia's Outback & Beto's Hot Sauce, 721
Cherry St., 940-549-1227

K Bob's Restaurant, 1111 Hwy 16 S, 940-549-3591

K & N Root Beer, 1108 South Elm Street, 940-549-
2247

Lake Country Pizza, Hwy 16 S, 940-549-8652

Last Action Hero Deli, 409 Third Street (west side
of Square), 940-549-3354

The Last Pizza Show, 526 Oak Street (west side of
Square), 940-549-5256

Magnolia Tea Room, 523 Fourth Street (north side
of Square), 940-549-8000

McDonalds Restuarant, 1405 Hwy 16 S, 940-549-5117

Moore's Family Restaurant, 111 N. FM 2353 Possum Kingdom Lake, 940-779-2933

Pizza Hut Restaurant, 1113 Hwy 16 S, 940-549-5401

Possum Port Restaurant, 1401 Hwy 16 S, 940-549-6603

Sanderson's Restaurant, 1324 Hwy 16 S, 940-549-8270

Sonic Drive In, 1217 Hwy 16 S, 940-549-4000

Sonny's BBQ, 1010 Fourth Street, 940-540-0113

Steer Bowl, 1444 Fourth Street, 940-549-6331

Subway Sandwiches & Salads, Hwy 16 S, 940-549-4649

Sumptin' Fishy, 1917 Hwy 16 S, 940-549-1898

Taco Mayo, 1219 Hwy 16 S, 940-549-6353

Third Street Grill, 610 Third Street, 940-549-7440

Whataburger Restaurant, 1228 Hwy 16 S, 940-549-3420

TEXAS FORTS TRAIL

FORT Griffin

From Fort Belknap, take Highway 380 west to Throckmorton.

Frontier history looms great in Throckmorton County, where Throckmorton was established in 1879 as the county seat. The old military road from Fort Belknap to Forts Phantom Hill and Chadbourne, a route followed by the Butterfield Overland Mail, ran through its southeast corner. The trail, made by Captain R. B. Marcy on his return from Santa Fe in 1849 and followed by hundreds of California-bound emigrants in the 1850s, ran nearer to the center of the county. Near the southern boundary of the county—the Throckmorton-Shackelford line—is the site of the Comanche Indian Reservation, where from 1855 to 1859 several hundred Comanche Indians were maintained and given a start on the white man's road. These

29

Indians were blamed for the atrocities of their wild kinsmen. The fury of the frontier white people was turned against them, and, like the agricultural Indians on the Brazos Reservation, they were moved to the Indian Territory in 1859. The presence of the Indian reservation and Camp Cooper brought a few settlers to the region, with the 1860 census recording 124 people in the area of Throckmorton County.

Near the Comanche Reservation, seven miles up the Clear Fork from Fort Griffin, was the military post of Camp Cooper. Established in 1856 to protect the Comanche Indian Reservation, it was the place Robert E. Lee called his Texas home. Lee was in command of the post from April 1856 to July 1857. The Civil War almost started at Camp Cooper. Weeks before Beauregard fired on Fort Sumter, Captain S. D. Carpenter, in command of Camp Cooper, defied an aggregation of Texans who demanded that the place be turned over to them. They were acting without the authority of any government, and no doubt soon would have attacked the post. Carpenter surely would have fought them if a contingent of Texas troops under Colonel W. C. Dalrymple had not arrived in time. Carpenter turned the post over to the state force.

From Throckmorton Highway 283 will lead straight south to old Fort Griffin.

Fort Griffin was located on a plateau eight hundred yards south of the Clear Fork of the Brazos and sixty feet above the valley. This position gave Griffin command of the area and discouraged any Indian attack unless the Indians had artillery! Lieutenant Colonel S. D. Sturgis, with four companies of the Sixth Cavalry, was quite pleased to leave behind old Fort Belknap and occupy the new site on July 31, 1867. It was not until June 3 of the following year that Lieutenant Colonel S. B. Hayman and companies of the Seventeenth Infantry arrived. The post was originally named Camp Wilson in memory of the son of the United States Senator from Massachusetts, but was shortly changed to Fort Griffin after General Charles Griffin, commander of the Military Department of Texas from 1866–67. (Rister 1956, 63–65)

A few days after the arrival of Colonel Sturgis, "Government Hill" as it was called, underwent dramatic change in preparation for construction of the post. Real progress began with the arrival of Lieutenant H. B. Mellen, acting quartermaster from San Antonio, with supplies and twenty-two carpenters, a building superintendent, masons, and sawyers. By winter Mellen had constructed a line of officers' quarters with a room and kitchen each, and forty-two small one-room log huts, 14'6" x 8' x 5'10", for the enlisted men. The latter would quarter six men.

The following year the men cut 1,025 logs of oak, elm, and cottonwood from which they milled 83,264 feet to build a hospital, post surgeon's quarters, commanding officer's quarters, kitchens, buildings for first sergeants, a stable, and other such buildings at a cost of $22,000. It seemed like a real bargain, but the lumber was green; it shrank and warped badly which allowed the cold winter winds and the spring sand storms to penetrate the quarters, making for miserable living conditions. The enlisted men's low morale was due to the poor condition of their

quarters. The cavalry mounts had it the worst, as only one stable had been constructed leaving most of the horses open to the elements and causing several of them to die from pneumonia. The original plans called for all the quarters ultimately to be built of stone, but the commissary, bakery, magazine, hospital, and commander's quarters were made of stone and wood. (Rister 1956, 67–68)

Because of its location Fort Griffin became one of the most strategic posts between Fort Richardson and the Big Bend. It provided troops for detached duty at the subposts of Belknap, Phantom Hill, and Mountain Pass (forty miles southwest of Phantom). Their primary duty was to provide armed escorts for the stagecoaches carrying mail and passengers along the trail, government supply trains, and surveying parties, and riding general patrol along the frontier. Even so, Indians and renegades found it easy to slip through the gaps in the defense line. (Rister 1956, 67–68)

Tonkawa scouts assisted the regular patrols sent out from Griffin, but it was a rare occasion that these patrols encountered hostiles. The lack of activity led the enlisted men to file complaints that claimed they were primarily being used as construction workers to improve the quarters of the officers. Thus Colonel Sturgis was quite pleased to order Captain Adna R. Chaffee to take the field on March 5, 1868, in pursuit of a band of Quahadi Comanches who were being led by a Mexican and a mulatto, following their raid on the Mill Creek Wagon Train. The Comanches, once they realized they were being pursued, split into two groups, and Chaffee chose to follow the warriors who had dared to strike a government wagon train so near the fort. He caught up with them at the Wichita River Breaks, and in the ensuing battle, Chaffee killed five Indians, the Mexican and the mulatto, captured five horses, and destroyed the village. (Rister 1956, 73–75)

In July of 1870, a force of thirty-seven enlisted men with Tonk scouts were sent in pursuit following a successful Comanche raid on local ranchers. The command caught up with the marauders west of Phantom Hill and recaptured the cattle. The troopers continued to pursue the Indians until the trail was wiped out by a buffalo stampede, a trick used quite often by the Indians to make good their escape. (Rister 1956, 75)

Life at Griffin was about to change, however. It became a center for Mackenzie's campaigns against the Indians in 1871, 1872 and 1874. On September 19, 1871, four companies of Mackenzie's Fourth Cavalry left Fort Richardson to take up quarters at Camp Cooper, and were joined by two companies each from Concho and Griffin and two companies of the Eleventh Infantry. Mackenzie and his command rode away on October 3 in fine spirits, singing, "Come home, John, don't stay long . . ." and returned in November after a semi-successful campaign.

The presence of Fort Griffin and Mackenzie's campaign gave the settlers of the region a false sense of security. The Indians continued to raid almost at will, and on June 9, 1872, White Horse hit the homestead of Able John Lee, killing him, his wife, and one daughter and taking captive Susanne, 17, John, 6, and Millie, 9. He then returned to their Rainy Mountain village across the Red River where the Lee children were given into slavery. Shortly afterwards Mackenzie again took the field, using Griffin as a supply base. This time when he returned to Griffin in November, he brought with him captives taken from Mow-way's camp. The whole village turned out to view the captives and to welcome the returning heroes. (Rister 1956, 94–96)

Although Mackenzie had been victorious the settlers felt that the Indians could still raid at will. However, the Quaker Indian Policy was under attack and would soon be repealed to allow the military to pursue marauding Indians. Indication of the impending change was seen when Lawrie Tatum refused to ransom the Lee children and threatened to cut off the Indian's rations until the children were returned. The Indians acquiesced, and the Lee children were given up. Even though the Tatum policy was proven to be effective the supporters of the Quaker Peace Policy were still in charge and Tatum, in ill health and under fire, resigned on March 31, 1873. He was replaced by James M. Hayworth, who managed to return the captive women and children at Concho to the reservation and to get the return of Satanta and Big Tree as well. Instead of this being a positive move toward peace the Indians took it as a victory, and the summer of 1873 saw the Indian marauders returning to the Texas frontier. (Rister 1956, 100–07)

As complaints poured into Washington from eastern Colorado, New Mexico and Texas about the increasing number of raids, it became evident that something had to be done. On the reservation the young chiefs and warriors were increasing their demand for war while the older braves were advising peace. Onto the scene came a Quahadi medicine man, Esa-tai, who supposedly had powers to raise the dead, produce cartridges from his stomach, and influence the white men so they would not injure the Indians. He proposed a two-pronged attack against the Fort Griffin Tonkawas and the buffalo hunters at Adobe Walls. Before the first could be carried out the Tonkawas were warned and moved into Fort Griffin. However, on June 27, 1874, about seven hundred braves hit the thirty-eight hunters at Adobe Walls. The Indians paid a high price for their attack and Esa-tai's medicine proved to be bad. (Rister 1956, 109–10)

Little did the Indians realize how bad the medicine of Esa-tai had been. It was the beginning of the end for them. Washington now ordered the Indians at the agency to declare for either peace or war, with those choosing the latter having to stay away from the agency. Fort Griffin became the center of activity as plans were made for a campaign against those Indians who chose war. For a brief period of time General C. C. Augur was at Griffin planning the campaign, and Lieutenant Colonel George Buell led out six companies of cavalry and two of infantry into the upper Brazos and Red River country. (Rister 1956, 111–13) It was also from Griffin that the Mackenzie Trail, famed in verse and story, ran 140 miles northwest to the mouth of Blanco Canyon. The campaign of 1874 and 1875 altered the life of Fort Griffin. The Indian wars moved further west, and the area around Griffin was rapidly settled.

The life of the enlisted men continued to be relatively drab. Their living quarters remained in poor condition. Their diet was made up of bacon, beans, and molasses, broken only occasionally by the presence of plum pudding and stewed dried apples. However, the boring routine of the post was broken by visiting the village below the hill, the town of Fort Griffin. Ultimately the post was closed on May 31, 1881.

The town of Fort Griffin quickly grew up around the fort and became a thriving trade center, with a reputation for crime and vice not altogether undeserved. During a period of twelve years thirty-five men were publicly killed there. The historian Carl Coke Rister wrote that "the revolver settled more differences than the judge," and added that straight shooting could promote long life more than fresh air and sunshine.

Business was generally good. Buffalo hunters, rich at least for a few hours after their arrival in town, made good customers. Cowboys and cattlemen found an oasis in the Bee Hive Saloon. ("In this hive we are All Alive; good whiskey makes us funny . . ."). Some visited other establishments that appealed to them.

In 1876 two major events happened to Fort Griffin. The first was the arrival from Fort Richardson of Lottie Deno, riding on top of the stage with the driver. Lottie took up residence in a Clear Fork shanty. An air of mystery developed about her, as she was seldom seen except when she visited the stores for supplies, or at night when she played cards at the Bee Hive or presided over the gambling room night after night. Her seclusion had everyone speculating. Some said she was kept by a prominent married saloon keeper. One day twenty-two-year-old Johnnie Golden arrived in Griffin. As the story goes Lottie fell for him and broke off her relationship with the saloon keeper. Shortly afterward Johnnie was arrested for horse stealing, but he never made it to the jail as a mob took him from the officers and killed him. Some say the saloon keeper paid $250 to dispose of Johnnie. Whatever the case, Lottie soon left Griffin, leaving the people as puzzled about her as they had been before. (Rister 1956, 135–38)

The second development of 1876 involved some enterprising Fort Griffin merchants. They sent a man to Belton where he sought to turn cattle herds away from the Chisholm toward the western or Dodge City cattle trail, which would bring business to Griffin. For several years thereafter herds aggregating 100,000 head and more passed this way annually. Meanwhile, merchants such as Frank Conrad and Charles Rath sold quantities of goods to buffalo hunters and people of the vicinity. With the closing of Fort Griffin, the town of Griffin soon dwindled, and by the end of the century only a combination general store and post office remained. It, too, would soon be abandoned.

TOURIST INFORMATION

(When possible please call ahead to be sure these services are still available.)

Fort Griffin State Historical Park

(915/762-3592) E-mail fgsp@camalott.com

Points of Interest:	Camping and hiking, nature trails, ball diamonds, amphitheatre, river walk, historic Fort Griffin, Texas Longhorn herd.
Annual Events:	March: Longhorn Calf Branding Historic Trail Ride April: Indian Wars Reenactment May: Memorial Day Weekend, Cowboy Campfire Breakfast June: Albany Fandangle July: Night Sky Viewing September: Labor Day Weekend, Cowboy Campfire Breakfast Fall: Civil War Reenactment, Night Sky Viewing December: 1870 Country Christmas

Throckmorton,

Chamber of Commerce, Box 711, Throckmorton, TX 76083
(817/849-2661)

Population:	1,054
Points of interest:	**1890 courthouse** **Old Jail House and Museum** **Putnam House** **Red Star Studio of sculptor Joe Barrington,** known for his out-sized creations in metal art
Annual Events:	June: Pioneer Days in odd years
Accommodations:	Cow Country Motel, 126 N. Minter

Andrews House, Bed and Breakfast, Eliasville, Texas, 817-362-4243

Prairie Bell Hotel, Woodson, Texas, 817-345-6599

Restaurants:

The Country Cafe, 102 Matthews Street

Rancher's Restaurant, 801 N. Minter

Woodson Inn, Hwy 183

Specialty
Shopping:

Ruby's Corner Store

*Continue along Highway 283 from Fort Griffin straight into **Albany.***

Albany became the county seat of Shackelford County in 1874, and soon overtook and passed Fort Griffin in population and business. Sallie Reynolds Matthews lived here, whose life story, along with that of the community, is related in a frontier classic, *Interwoven*. The title comes from the intermarriage of members of two outstanding families of the county, Matthews and Reynolds.

Albany's awareness of its past is immediately noticeable in the historical preservation in the town. Also Albany produces the "Fort Griffin Fandangle" each year, an historical pageant put on by home talent. In the early 1930s, Robert Nail, a Princeton graduate in drama and a Phi Beta Kappa, began to apply his talent to the

fascinating story of the Clear Fork country frontier. Through the years he made the production an event of renown. Since his death his associates have continued this fine production.

While you are in the neighborhood you might want to take a short detour east along Highway 180 and visit Lake Hubbard and Breckenridge which was the center of the oil boom in this part of Texas.

*From Albany head west along Highway 180 to FM 600, and then proceed south to **Fort Phantom Hill**.*

On approaching the post you will see the remaining chimneys standing like sentinels on what looks like a formidable hill overlooking the Clear Fork of the Brazos. As one nears the hill it disappears and becomes a gentle slope, barely perceptible when one arrives; thus one of the stories of how the post got its name. A second account has to do with a nervous sentry firing on what he thought was an Indian on the hill. A following investigation failed to discover the presence of any Indians, and one of the troopers suggested that the man had seen a ghost. Whatever the case, Major General Persifor F. Smith, commanding the Fifth Military Department (Texas), in General Orders Number 91 ordered a post established "at, or in the immediate vicinity of, a point known as Phantom Hill" on the Clear Fork of the Brazos. (Richardson 1963, 68)

Major J. J. Abercrombie was given the task and arrived on the scene on November 14, 1851. His introduction to the region was not kind, as exposure to a wet norther cost him one teamster and twenty horses, mules, and oxen—all frozen to death. Not only was the environment hostile, but Major Abercrombie soon discovered that the site had been chosen from an earlier survey on the assumption that the needs for the construction and maintenance of a post—wood and water—were available. He immediately reported to his superiors that neither wood for construction nor water suitable for men or animals was to be had. Unfortunately, General Smith had left the field to escort an ill General Belknap to Fort Washita, and could not be contacted for several weeks. There was no one who could change the orders. Abercrombie had to make the best of a bad situation, and construction of Fort Phantom Hill began.

The hardships of surviving that first winter are well described by Lieutenant Clinton W. Lear in a series of letters to his wife in New Orleans. Somewhat of a romantic, Lieutenant Lear was taken by the beauty of the area with its abundant fish, deer, wild turkeys, and bear. He felt it unfortunate that such a beautiful place had so little to offer a military post. He said that he spent most of his time searching for timber—the best stand for construction purposes was six miles away. The winter of 1851–1852 was spent in tents, pitched in a grove of black jacks. The most immediate problem— water—was solved when a spring was found nearby, but it disappeared during the dry summer. A well of good water was dug some four miles from the site. (Richardson 1963, 89–91)

With the coming of summer a permanent post was begun, when a good stone quarry was located on the east bank of Elm Creek about two miles distant, and with the arrival of a stone mason. A stone storehouse, creditable stone quarters for the commanding officer, a hospital of rude logs, and a half dozen or more quarters for officers built principally of logs (jacal huts of upright poles interlaced with bough and daubed with mud) were built.

Fort Phantom Hill was garrisoned by Companies B, C, E, G, and K of the Fifth Infantry. The plans called for one hundred horses to mount one company of infantry for scouting. The military failed to understand at the time that putting an infantryman on a horse did not make a cavalry. That problem, however, was not Abercrombie's as he was transferred out on April 27, 1852, and was replaced by Lieutenant Colonel Carlos A. Waite. On September 23, 1853, four companies were transferred out to be replaced by Company I of the Second Dragoons, bringing post strength to 139 men. Major H. H. Sibley took command of the post then, but only stayed until March of 1854, when he was replaced by Lieutenant N. C. Givens. Lieutenant Givens' command was short-lived, as the troops finally shook the dust of Fort Phantom Hill from their shoes when they marched out on April 6, 1854. (Richardson 1963, 92–95)

Life at Fort Phantom Hill had been arduous for the men. The lack of a post garden, which created a shortage of vegetables in the men's diet, led to scurvy, intermittent fever, dysentery, colds, and pneumonia. Nor were necessities provided by settlers in the area, as happened at most posts, because there were no settlers, and no town had grown up around the fort. The only break in the monotony of fort life was excursions into the field, which meant extended marches across arid land with inadequate supplies of food and water.

Shortages prevailed in all areas of the life of Fort Phantom Hill, from uniforms to arms. Fortunately the men were not engaged in hostile action, although it was reported that Indians did visit the post where they made a general nuisance of themselves. The post did receive a major scare when Buffalo Hump's tribe of 2,500 passed by the fort. The men were placed in battle array as soon as the Northern Comanche tribe was spotted. Whether the

Indians would have attacked the post is speculative, for once they saw the preparations, they passed it by with scowls and angry looks. One arrogant Northern Comanche did send Major Sibley a message that "when grass became good again he was coming down and whip him." (Richardson 1963) The Indian never came.

One final story of interest regarding Fort Phantom Hill deals with who burned the post. There are three versions of its destruction. One says that it was burned by trooper Scullion and a slave who slipped back the first night after abandonment because of their distaste for the post. A second has the Indians destroying the post, while a third says that it was destroyed by Confederate troops. All that is known for sure is that by November 9, 1854 when Charles A. Crosby camped there it had been burned. (Rister 1938, 9. Richardson 1963, 95)

The withdrawal of the military did not mean the end of occupants of Fort Phantom Hill. In 1858, a Mr. Burlington and his wife operated a stage station for the Butterfield line until it was abandoned during the Civil War. After the war Fort Phantom Hill became a subpost of Fort Griffin. Accordingly, on June 5, 1871, Captain Theodore Schwan and Company G of the Eleventh Infantry were sent to Fort Phantom to protect the traffic through

Magazine.

the area, and to provide a detail of one noncommissioned officer and six men to guard the mail station at Mountain Pass, the first stop south of Phantom Hill. In 1874, a detachment from the fort was engaged by a force of seventy-five Comanches and Kiowas. Following a brief battle of one and a half hours the Indians broke off hostilities, with six killed and several wounded. (Rister 1938, 11–12)

As hostiles moved further west and thousands of immigrants began to settle in West Texas the troopers left Phantom, but in their place grew a thriving frontier town of Phantom Hill, complete with hotel, saloons, gambling halls, and various shops. When Jones County was created it was hoped that Phantom would become the county seat, but it lost out to Anson. It was not long before Phantom was once again abandoned. (Rister 1938)

Today the remains of the fort are located on private land. The owner is doing his best to restore some parts of the post and to make it a pleasant stop for travelers. It is interesting to note that Fort Phantom Hill was originally built on land that had been sold on August 3, 1851, to A. C. Daws for fifty dollars and the only reason that it did not create a problem was its isolation. The old powder magazine to the west of the road still stands, as well as the post guard house. A part of the stone commissary can still be seen on the east side of the fort, and of course the chimneys still stand like sentries on the prairie. A poem written by ranch poet Larry Chittenden fully catches the spirit of Phantom in the first stanza which reads:

On the breezy Texas border, on the prairies far away
Where the antelope is grazing and the Spanish ponies play;
Where the tawny cattle wander through the golden incensed hours,
And the sunlight woos a landscape clothed in royal robes of flowers;

Where the Elm and Clear Fork mingle, as they journey to
    the sea,
And the night-wind sobs sad stories o'er a wild and lonely
    lea;
Where of old the dusky savage and the shaggy bison trod,
And the reverent plains are sleeping 'midst drowsy dreams
    of God;
Where the twilight loves to linger, e'er night's sable robes
    are cast
'Round grim-ruined, spectral chimneys, telling stories of
    the past,
There upon an airy mesa, close beside a whispering rill
There to-day you'll find the ruins of Old Fort Phantom Hill.
(Rister 1938, 13)

From Fort Phantom Hill continue south along FM 600 to Abilene. Along the way you will pass Lake Fort Phantom which provides Abilene with a large part of its water supply.

Abilene had its beginning in 1880 in a meeting at the Hashknife Ranch headquarters, located just north of present Thirteenth Street on the bluff overlooking Cedar Creek. Cattlemen and railroad men broke bread together at this meeting and reached some important decisions whereby the ranchers agreed to provide the railroad with land for a depot, sidings, and cattle loading pens at half the base price of $1.50 per acre. The railroad would also be responsible for laying out the town, arranging publicity, and staging an auction. (Downs, 1981, 3–4) H. C. Withers represented the Texas and Pacific Railroad Company, John N. Simpson was one of the spokesmen for regional cattlemen. Among several other persons in the group, an important one was Sam L. Chalk, a surveyor. C. W. Merchant named the town after Abilene, Kansas, to which he had driven cattle. In their publicity the railroad people and also residents of the embryonic town referred to it as the "Future Great City of West Texas," and their successors have never disclaimed the title.

The Texas and Pacific Railroad reached Abilene in early 1881, and by the time of the auctioning of town lots on March 15, a tent city of 300 people had sprung up. On the first day of the auction 139 lots were sold for $27,000. From that point on the town began to carve out its future in northeast Taylor County. In 1883, in a hotly contested vote with Buffalo Gap, Abilene won the county seat. It rapidly became the center of the county and indeed the larger Big Country—the area within a 75 to 100 mile radius of Abilene.

The city became a shipping point for buffalo bones, cattle, sheep, and various agricultural products. It soon boasted two newspapers and several churches, and in 1890 the foundation of the first of three Christian universities to be located in the city was laid. The first was Simmons College, later Hardin-Simmons University, followed in 1920 by Abilene Christian College when Childers Classical Institute, founded in 1906, officially changed its name. In 1923, McMurry College was established. Abilene was never a boisterous town, even though the city has placed a marker on the spot where John J. Clinton, long-time police and fire chief of Abilene, discharged his six-shooter at midnight each New Year's Eve as a curfew closing all saloons and reminding trigger-happy cowboys and gunmen to desist.

Abilene's major boom period came during World War II with the establishment of Camp Barkeley, 1941–1945, and the Army Air Base at Tye in 1943. Barkeley was originally designed to hold twenty thousand men, but was expanded to a capacity of fifty thousand plus a prisoner of war camp. Approximately one and a half million men passed through Barkeley, and Abilene was never quite the same. With the ending of the war Abilene suffered the same readjustment that all military towns had gone through, but it did better than most when it secured Dyess Air Force Base in 1955. Today Abilene has an economy solidly based in agriculture, education, military, and a multitude of small and intermediate industries which help keep things going during the boom and bust cycles experienced by Abilene's oil community. The latest civic development of Abilene's leadership has been the creation of the Grace Cultural Center located downtown.

Ten miles south of Abilene on County Road 89 is **Buffalo Gap**, *a pass through the Callahan Divide which looms clearly. Off to the southwest, East Peak and Castle Peak can be seen in the distance, standing out from the main escarpment of the mesa. These peaks were well-known markers to the pioneers along the old military road and stage line of the 1850s. Beyond Castle Peak (called Abercrombie Peak by the early military men) a few miles is Mountain Pass, site of a Butterfield stage stand.*

Some distance northeast of Castle Peak, in the vicinity of present Dyess Air Force Base, Major George H. Thomas, on an August day in 1860, returning from an extended scout for hostile Indians came across a fresh Indian trail and gave pursuit. Some forty-five miles to the northwest his contingent of the Second Cavalry sighted the Indians, and a chase began. When the troops were about to overtake the Comanches, an old warrior decided that they would have to be delayed and that he was expendable. He dismounted, probably removed his moccasins as a token that he would not leave the place, and as the excited troops dashed up, greeted them with a stream of arrows. Two of the barbed dogwood switches wounded the commander severely, and five troopers were wounded—all with arrows or a spear. Through an interpreter Thomas tried to get the Comanche to surrender, but the warrior scoffed at the suggestion and taunted the "long knives" to come and get him. At last the troops killed him and found some twenty wounds on his body. With his primitive weapons he had de-

Commanding officer's quarters.

layed a score or more of well-armed troops, permitting his companions to escape.

Buffalo Gap got its name from trails made during the centuries by myriads of bison as they passed through the gap in the Callahan Divide. Its great old oaks and lasting water made the gap a favorite camping place for Indians and buffalo hunters alike. It may have come within the orbit of European exploration at a very early date, for there is substantial evidence that the Spanish explorer Francisco Vasquez de Coronado spent some time in this vicinity in 1541. Guided by Comanche Chief Soxias and his party, Jose Mares came through Buffalo Gap in 1788 on his way from San Antonio to Santa Fe. One branch of the Western (Dodge City) Cattle Trail came through Buffalo Gap and Abilene. The noted cattleman/author Andy Adams has recorded that in looking northwest from a hill near the Gap on an occasion in the early 1880s, he counted nine herds of cattle, each containing at least a thousand head.

It was the hunters that first began to establish themselves in what is today Buffalo Gap, to take advantage of the passing buffalo herds. Visitors recalled seeing stacks of buffalo hides piled twenty feet high in the streets. Cattlemen arrived later, and the first stores in Buffalo Gap were opened in 1877. The community received mail twice weekly from Eastland, some fifty miles to the east. The next year Taylor County was organized, and by 1880 Buffalo Gap had 1,200 citizens and had become the county seat.

Unfortunately, the future growth of Buffalo Gap was cut short when the T&P chose to build its own town—Abilene. That town quickly grew and in 1882 won the election to become the county seat. However, it took the Texas Rangers to get Buffalo Gap to relinquish the county records. It was not long until the Gap became a village only to be disturbed by the arrival of the Santa Fe Railroad. The Santa Fe did not change the Gap much, although it did add to its economic development. Perhaps a more sensational development took place in 1965 when the people of Buffalo Gap voted 76–75 to allow the sale of alcoholic beverages—a second such development in an all-dry Taylor County.

Today visitors to Buffalo Gap will find it still a village nestled among the oaks. The two-story county jail constructed of native stone blocks and mortised together with cannonballs brought from Civil War battlefields stands as an anchor in the Buffalo Gap Historic Village. The Historic Village is a project taken on by Dr. Lee Rode. It is one of the best locally developed historic sites in the state. Dr. Rode has collected such buildings as a doctor's and dentist's office, a railroad depot, a log cabin, a country church (which is used by many young people for their weddings), print shops, and barns filled with all types of western relics such as wagons.

From Buffalo Gap take County Road 613 to Tuscola.

Started in 1881 by Dr. Clarence M. Cash, an early-day Taylor County physician, the town was named in honor of his home town: Tuscola, Illinois. With the coming of the Abilene and Southern, and the Gulf, Colorado, and Santa

Fe railroads in the early twentieth century, the hamlet became a town.

Traveling south along U. S. Highway 83 from **Tuscola** *to* **Winters,** *you will see Bald Eagle Peak, with an elevation of 2,250 feet. It was a landmark for pioneers and the beginning point of some early-day land survey.*

"Winters is like Topsy, she just growed," states an authority on the history of the town. Winters is located on the rolling plains of West Texas in Runnels County. It was in 1880 that the C. N. Curry and C. E. Bell families settled in the area. In 1889 Mr. J. N. Winters, a rancher and land agent, donated land on which a school house stood. The following year during a meeting in the school house the people voted to name the town for Mr. Winters. The town was chartered in 1894. By 1901 the community had a string band, a brass band, and a band wagon drawn by four white horses. The railroad arrived in 1909, which gave the local agri-economy a boost, while the discovery of oil in 1949 helped the industrial growth of the area.

Officers' quarters.

FORT
Chadbourne

From Winters head west along Highway 153, then northwest on 153 by Wingate to U. S. Highway 77. Go southwest here for a few miles and you will pass the site of **Fort Chadbourne.** The site, a half mile to the southeast of the road, is on private land, and the owner has basically closed the site to the public.
(continued next page)

Fort Chadbourne, established in October 1852, by Companies A and K of the Eighth U. S. Infantry, was named for Lieutenant Theodore L. Chadbourne who was killed at the Battle of Rasaca de la Palma during the Mexican War. The fort served as a station on the Butterfield Overland Mail line and remained an active post for almost a decade before federal troops abandoned the site on March 23, 1861, on the eve of the Civil War. The site was then taken over by Henry E. McCulloch, commissioner for Texas. Following a six-year absence United States troops reoccupied the post for a short period after the war, beginning on May 25, 1867, and concluding the following December.

51

Alternate Route: You may wish to bypass the post and follow U. S. Highway 83 from Winters to Ballinger and thence along U. S. Highway 67 to San Angelo.

Various military units occupied Fort Chadbourne between 1852 and 1867, including elements of the Eighth United States Infantry, the Second United States Dragoons, the Texas Mounted Volunteers (portions of which were mustered at the post in March 1855), the First United States Infantry, the Second United States Cavalry, and the Fourth United States Cavalry. (Bitner 1933, 8)

Among the more notable figures who served at the post prior to the Civil War were Lieutenants James Longstreet, Arthur Pendleton Bagley, and George E. Pickett, each of whom became distinguished Confederate generals during the Civil War. Miles W. Keogh was also posted to Fort Chadbourne during its brief reoccupation in 1867. He, as captain in the Seventh United States Cavalry, was destined to fall at the Battle of Little Big Horn some nine years later on June 25, 1876. (Crimmins 1950, 444–45 1933, Bitner, 1933 7–8).

The site selected for the post was near Oak Creek, a small tributary of the Colorado River. According to the federal War Department, the fort was established to provide protection from hostile Indians. At this time the fort was in an isolated location, as Colonel J. K. F. Mansfield noted in his inspection report of 1856:

> The country about here is not particularly inviting to settlers and I should think on account of the generally poor land and dry seasons, it will not soon be occupied. There are no settlements unconnected with the garrison directly or indirectly. (Crimmins 1939, 369)

Three years earlier in August of 1853, Colonel W. G. Freeman, also conducting an inspection of the post noted in his report that even though a direct road connected Fort Chadbourne with Fort

Mason, 120 miles to the southeast, no communications had existed with Fort Phantom Hill to the north. At the time of Freeman's inspection the two forts, situated only fifty-nine miles from one another, had coexisted in the region for eleven months. In fact, the trail connecting the two posts was so indistinct and difficult to follow that Freeman's guide to Fort Phantom Hill, an original explorer of the route, became temporarily lost on the journey. (Crimmins 1950, 443, 448)

The land around Fort Chadbourne is for the most part rolling prairie. An abundance of lime and sandstone existed in the vicinity of the fort for construction purposes, as well as scrub oak for timber. Some buildings at the fort, such as the barracks and hospital, were of stone construction with shingled roofs. Others, such as the bakery, granary, adjutant's office, commissary's office, and some officers' quarters were log buildings. The semi-arid nature of the land was detrimental to the post's water supply, which during the dry season was in limited quantity and of poor quality. (Crimmins 1950, 443–44; Crimmins 1939, 365, 367–68)

As a military outpost Fort Chadbourne was in the heart of the Peneteka Comanche country and much of its history is associated with those natives. Although nominally at peace with the whites certain chiefs such as Sanaco and Buffalo Hump could not be trusted, and frequently bands of warriors would escape the control of their tribal leaders. On one occasion some passengers on the Butterfield stage witnessed a band of Comanches rustling a small herd of horses, in complete disregard to the presence of nearby troops. In 1854 Indians killed a Captain Van Buren in the vicinity. Sometime later renegade Comanches caught two soldiers serving as mail carriers, tied them to a tree, and burned them. Future general David M. Stanley related how one soldier managed to reach the post after an Indian attack, even though fourteen arrows protruded from him, making him look like a porcupine. A doctor subsequently removed the arrows and within two weeks the soldier was again walking around.

Stanley also related how Major Seth Eastman, who commanded the post, invited a band of Comanches into the garrison in an attempt to take them prisoner since he believed some forty members of this group were responsible for committing atrocities. Eastman pow-wowed with the Indians in an effort to stall them while a contingent of troops being drilled were deployed to surround the band. It was not the practice of Plains Indians to surrender and a number of them were killed in the attempt to capture them. The only enduring result of the ruse was the destruction of the red men's confidence in the soldiers.

Fortunately, not all relations between the races at Fort Chadbourne had to do with tomahawk and rifle. When the wife of post surgeon Dr. Ebenezer Swift gave birth to a baby boy the squaws formed a line to see the white child. They called the infant *Chiquito Medico,* Little Doctor—many Texas Comanches spoke limited Spanish.

In his book *Our Wild Indians* Colonel Richard M. Dodge, who knew the Old West from experience, attaches to Fort Chadbourne a tale told throughout the Great Plains frontier. Indians were fond of both horse racing and gambling and not infrequently officers and troops stationed at the various frontier posts would engage in some competition with them. On one particular occasion a band of Comanches under Mu-la-que-top camped near Fort Chadbourne. During the course of their stay some officers from the post challenged the Indians to a bit of horse racing. The Indians accepted the challenge with the result that their somewhat inferior and often pathetic looking entry bested a magnificent Kentucky mare owned by one of the soldiers. The Comanche rider added insult to financial injury by riding the last fifty yards of the race mounted face to tail, beckoning the rider of the mare to come on. (Dodge 1883, 341–42)

In March 1861, on the threshold of the Civil War, federal troops abandoned Fort Chadbourne and did not reoccupy the post until May 25, 1867, following the conclusion of hostilities, when elements of the Fourth United States Cavalry returned to Chadbourne. By late June, a rapid buildup of military personnel at the post resulted in an overall troop strength of 331. Lieutenant Colonel Eugene B. Beaumont received orders to take command, assisted by Major Michael J. Kelly. In July further reinforcement of the Fourth Cavalry arrived from Camp Verde under Captain G. G. Huntt, who then assumed command of the post. (Haley 1952, 122; Bitner 1933, 8)

Following the war, the first operations out of Fort Chadbourne revolved around providing escort and protection for the cattle herds traveling the Goodnight Trail. The increased activity on the trail in the spring and summer of 1867 was followed by a corresponding escalation in Indian raids. This ultimately resulted in the military posting 423 men to Chadbourne. Though these troops provided some security they were not located where protection was most urgently needed. By November the establishment of Camp Hatch (later named Fort Concho), at a more practical geographic point fifty miles to the south, marked the end of Fort Chadbourne. Following the abandonment of the garrison in late November and early December of 1867 its usefulness for the next year was then relegated to that of a picket post. (Haley 1952, 122–29; Bitner 1933, 8)

*From Fort Chadbourne continue along U. S. Highway 277 to **Bronte** and then on to **San Angelo**.*

Bronte was established in 1887 and named for the English novelist, Charlotte Brontë. Apparently someone in the community at that time was an admirer of the author of *Jane Eyre*.

*West of Bronte on Highway 158 is **Robert Lee**.*

Established in 1889 by L. S. Harris and R. E. Cartlege, these Confederate veterans named the town after the great hero of the South. In 1891, Robert Lee won the county seat of Coke County in a contest with Hayrick.

TOURIST INFORMATION

(When possible please call to be sure these services are still available.)

Albany (915/762-2525)

Chamber of Commerce, P. O. Box 185, Albany, TX 76430

Population:	2,040
Points of interest:	**Shackelford County Court House**, built in 1883–84

The square

Old Jail Art Center, on Second Street one block east of the the courthouse, permanent exhibits include works of Giacomo Manzu, John Marin, Charles Umlauf, Louise Nevelson, Henry Moore, Amedeo Modigliani, Pablo Picasso, and examples of Chinese art from the Han, Wei, Sui, Tang and Ming Dynasties. Housed in a restored county jail (c. 1878). Open Tuesday–Saturday from 10–5, Sunday from 2–5.

Ledbetter Picket House, 700 Railroad Street, restored frontier dog-run cabin built of slender upright poles (pickets), with rustic period furnishings. Open daily from 8–5.

Matthews Memorial Presbyterian Church, built in 1898 and housing one of the finest pipe organs in West Texas

Old MKT Depot, Central and Main Streets, serves as chamber of commerce office, community center and exhibit area for local handicrafts. Open weekdays.

Georgia Monument, at South Main and South First Streets, erected in 1976 to honor the Georgia Battalion that volunteered in Texas's war for independence in 1836. Most were killed in the Goliad massacre.

Annual events:

April: 3rd Saturday, Polo on the Prairie; Discover Albany Day

June: the last two weekends, Fort Griffin Fandangle, presented by more than 200 townfolk, in an outdoor musical pageant depicting area history. The production is noted for its live longhorn herd on stage, a steam train, a calliope, an overland stage and team of mules, and an opening parade of flag-bearing riders on horseback.

September: 3rd Saturday, City-wide garage sale

October: 3rd Saturday, Cowboy Days

November: Matthews Memorial Presbyterian Church Bazaar; Holiday Preview

December: Albany Nativity, in even years

Accommodations:

Albany Motor Inn, 915-762-2451

Ann's (B&B), 915-762-3200

The Foreman's Cottage (B&B), Musselman Ranch, 915-762-2224

Hereford Motel, Hwy 80 W, 915-762-2451

The Lodge, 915-762-3205

The Old Nail House Inn (B&B), 915-762-2928

Virginia's (B&B), 915-762-2013

Restaurants:

Fort Griffin General Merchandise Restaurant, Hwy 80 W, 915-762-9034

Halberts Country Emporium, 211 S. Main St., 915-762-2977

High Lonesome Cafe, 915-762-2511

Icehouse, 915-762-3287

Lone Star Eatery, 915-762-2932

Specialty
Shopping:

Albany News, 915-762-2201
Blanton-Caldwell, 915-762-2370
Desperados, 915-762-3033
Erline's, 915-762-3083
Griffin Flat, 915-762-2009
Halbert's Country Emporium, 915-762-2977
Lynch Line, 915-762-2212
Main Street Mercantile, 915-762-3030
Outlaws Trading Post, 915-762-2687
Ranch Rags, 915-762-3000
Tenovus, 915-762-2898
House of Embroidery, 915-762-3073

Abilene 915/800-727-7704

Population:

110,661

Lakes:

Fort Phantom, Lytle, Kirby, and Abilene

Universities:

Abilene Christian University, Hardin-Simmons University, McMurry University, Cisco Junior College, Texas State Technical College

Points of interest:

Abilene State Park, fifteen miles southwest on FM 89, has camping, trailer facilities, picnicking, shelters, swimming pool, rest rooms and showers, hiking and fishing. A large grove of some 4,000 native pecan trees was once a popular campground for Comanche Indians. Admission.

Abilene State School

Abilene Zoo is one of the five largest in the state. Open daily from 10–5 (7 P.M. holidays and weekends in summer)

Camp Barkeley, Chimneys and foundations are all that remain of a WWII Army camp, located on Hwy. 277 between FM 1235 and FM 707 at the Historical Marker sign. The camp once housed over 60,000 men and a prisoner-of-war facility. Adjoining the Camp was Tye Field-Abilene Air Base, a training command for fighter pilots.

Center for Contemprary Arts, 220 Cypress, working artists have studios displaying rotating exhibits. Open Tuesday–Friday from 11–5, Saturday and Sunday from 1–4.

Dyess Air Force Base and Linear Air Park, Strategic Air Command base, home of the B-1 Bomber and training center for its crews, Loop 312 south of Business Loop I-20/U.S. 84. Dyess Linear Air Park of vintage aircraft includes World War II, Korean War, Vietnam War planes. Open during daylight hours. Visitors must stop at main entrance for a temporary pass. For extensive base tours to flight lines, reservations must be prearranged with Public Affairs office, 915-696-5609.

Frost Center for the Arts, Hardin-Simmons University, 2200 Hickory, 915-670-1246

West Texas Rehabilitation Center

Museums of Abilene are located in the historic Grace Hotel, known as the Grace Cultural Center, 102 Cypress Street. The Grace, built in 1909, is listed in the National Register of Historic Places; portions are restored to its 1929 condition. The museums are comprised of Abilene Fine Arts Museum, Abilene Historical Museum and the Children's Museum, National Center for Children's Illustrated Literature. Free admission on Thursday 5–8:30 P.M.

Open Tuesday–Saturday 10–5, Sunday 1–5. Admission.

Paramount Theatre, located downtown, is listed on the National Register of Historic Places. Created in the Spanish-Moorish revised mission style, the interior of the Paramount has a lobby with arched columns, two grand staircases, hand-blown glass chandeliers, and Pueblo-Deco artwork on the ceiling. The 1,200 seat auditorium features Moorish towers with domed turrets flanking the stage. Slowly drifting clouds and twinkling stars adorn the velvet blue sky. Self-guided tour.

Ryan Center of Fine Arts, McMurry University, S. 14th & Sayles Blvd., 915-691-6295

Shore Art Gallery, Abilene Christian University, 1600 Campus Ct, 915-674-2779

T & P Depot Visitors Center

Annual events:

Monthly: Art Walk, Second Thursday of each month, 5–8:30 P.M., 915-677-8389

January: Rehab Telethon, MHA Professional Tennis Tournament

February: Big Country Outdoor Sports Show; West Texas Arts and Crafts Show

April: 1st Weekend, Railroad and Art Festival; 2nd weekend, Rock Hound Roundup; 3rd Weekend, West Texas film Festival; Dyess Air Force Base Open House

May: Western Heritage Classic Ranch Rodeo features ranch rodeo, campfire cook-off, sheep dog trials, farrier competition, Cowboy Poet's Society, Western art show

June: Texas Double Trouble Bicycle Tour; Abilene Sunburn Grand Prix

July: Texas Cowboy Reunion & Rodeo, Stamford, Texas; 4th July Altrusa Antique Show; Abilene Shoot Out Drag racing

August: KeyCity Truckers West Texas Nationals

September: West Texas Fair, ten days in mid-September features exhibits and amusements; Chili Super Bowl Cook-off; Altrusa Antique Show

October: Big Country Renaissance Days, 1st and 2nd weekend; Gatlin Brothers Senior Southwest Classic Golf Tournament; West Texas Fair and Rodeo; Abilene Shoot-out Drag Racing

November: 1st weekend, Christmas in November

December: 1st Tuesday, Christmas parade and lighting

Accommodations: Alamo Motel, 2957 S. 1st, 915-676-7149

Antilley Inn, 6555 Hwy. 83-84, 915-695-3330

Bed and Breakfast Abilene Style, 4073 Caldwell Rd., 915-677-9677

Best Western South Mall, 3950 Ridgemont Drive, 915-695-1262

Blue Willow Bed & Breakfast, 435 College Drive, 915-677-8420

Bolin's Prairie House Bed & Breakfast, 508 Mulberry, 915-675-5855

Century Lodge, 3509 S, 1st, 915-677-8557

D & L Motel, 358 S. 11th, 915-672-0044

Days Inn, 1702 E. IH-20, 915-672-6433; 800-DaysInn

EconoLodge, 1622 W. Stamford, 915-673-5424; 800-446-6900

Embassy Suites, 4250 Ridgemont Drive, 915-698-1234; 800-Embassy

Great Western Inn, 1650 IH-20 East, 915-677-2200

Holiday Inn Express, 1625 Hwy. 351, 915-673-5271;
  800-Holiday

Kiva Inn, 5403 S. 1st, 915-695-4466; 800-592-4466

Lamplighter Motor Inn, 3153 S. 1st, 915-673-4251

La Quinta Inn, 3501 West Lake Rd., 915-676-1676;
  800-531-5900

Motel 6, 4951 W. Stamford, 915-672-8462

Ponca Motel, 3101 S. 1st, 915-673-9682

Quality Inn, 505 Pine, 915-676-0222; 800-588-0222

Ramada Inn, 3450 S. Clack, 915-695-7700; 800-2-
  Ramada

Red Carpet Inn, 2202 IH-20, 915-677-2463

Royal Inn, 5695 S. 1st, 915-692-3022; 800-588-4Fun

Super 8, IH-20 & Hwy. 351, 915-673-5251; 800-800-
  8000

Thurderbird Lodge, 840 E. Business 20, 915-677-
  8100; 800-880-7666

Tower Motel, 3417 S. 1st, 915-672-7849

Western Motel, 3201 S. 1st, 915-672-7858

Restaurants: Arby's 3824 S. Clack, 915-695-4491; 125 S. Pioneer,
  695-1710

Bar-B-Q Barn, Houston Street, 915-572-3552

Briarstone Drivateria, 2626 N. 1st, 915-673-8151

Burger King, 3901 N. 1st, 915-677-5917; 3650 S.
  Clack, 695-7961

Burgers and Fries, 4458 Buffalo Gap Road, 915-695-
  2888; 3373 S. 14th, 695-1847

Cahoots Catfish & Oyster Bar, 301 S. 11th, 915-672-
  6540

Casa Herrera, 4109 Ridgemont Drive, 915-692-7065

Catfish Corner, 780 S. Treadaway, 915-672-3620

Chick-Fil-A, Mall of Abilene, 915-695-2946

Chili's Grill & Bar, 4302 S. Clack, 915-698-1660

China Star, 3601 S. 1st, 915-677-2000

Chinese Kitchen, 3398 N. 1st, 915-676-2231

CiCi's Pizza, 3366 Turner Plaza, 915-692-1660

Dairy Queen, 601 Butternut, 915-677-4121; 2666 Pine, 673-9281; 942 N. Mockingbird, 673-0896; 302 S. Pioneer, 698-1691; 802 E. Business 20, 672-1251; 1102 S. Treadaway, 677-1611; 4157 Buffalo Gap Rd., 698-8182; 5110 S. Hwy. 277, 695-0332; State Hwy. 351, 677-0406

Dos Amigos, 3650 N. 6th, 915-672-2992

El Chico, Mall of Abilene, 915-695-2875

Cypress Street Station, 158 Cypress, 915-676-3463

Furr's Cafeteria, 3350 S. Clack, 915-692-8330

Garcia's, 3114 S. Clack, 915-691-9218

Golden Corral, 4100 S. Danville, 915-692-4592

Harlow's Smokehouse, 2002 N. Clack, 915-672-2132

Harlows South Forty, 542 E. S. 11th

Harold's Pit Bar-B-Q, 1305 Walnut, 915-672-4451

Joe Allen's Barbecue, 1233 S. Treadaway, 915-672-6082

Kentucky Fried Chicken, 3856 S. Clack, 915-695-3090

Kettle Restaurant, 3374 Turner Plaza, 915-692-4280; 1750 E. I-20, 672-4545

Little Caesar's Pizza, 4460 Buffalo Gap Road, 915-598-5252; 1035 N. Judge Ely, 677-2442; 3301 S. 14th, 692-0292

Luby's Cafeteria, Mall of Abilene, 915-695-2000

Mama Ruth's Diner, 1232 Grape, 915-672-1713

Miz Scarlett's Garden, 540 Grape, 915-671-9444

Olive Garden, 3210 S. Clack, 915-691-0388

The Outpost, 3126 S. Clack, 915-692-3595

Perini Ranch Steakhouse, Hwy. 89-Buffalo Gap, 915-572-3339

Pizza Inn, 849 E. Business 20, 915-672-5671

Red Lobster, 1280 S. Clack, 915-695-1191

Ronnie Ingle Pit Bar-B-Q, 3910 S. Treadaway, 915-695-9924

Schlotzsky's, 289 N. Judge Ely, 915-677-9127; 4613 S. 14th, 695-2021

Square's Bar-B-Que Express, 210 N. Leggett, 915-672-6752; 4592 Buffalo Gap Rd., 695-7933

Taco Bell, 925 Ambler, 915-673-9621; 3509 N. 1st, 672-5491; 1009 N. Judge Ely, 676-9362; 2901 S. 14th, 692-2436; 4165 S. Danville, 695-4900

Tucson's, 3370 N. 1st, 915-676-8279

Turnerhill's House of Bar-B-Que, 1881 N. Treadaway, 915-672-5811

Weekdays, 427 Pine, 915-672-3820

Wes-T-Go Truck Stop, I-20 West @ Tye, 915-692-6625

Western Sizzlin' Steakhouse, 1802 S. Clack, 915-698-4340

Wyatt's Cafeteria, 1026 N. Judge Ely, 915-675-6660

Zentner's Daughter Steakhouse, 4358 Sayles, 915-695-4290

Specialty Shopping:

Abilene Antique Galleria, 234 Chestnut, 915-673-8759

Antique & Almost, 3146 S. 11th, 915-695-2423

Antique Gallery, 2544 Barrow, 915-692-2422

Barnard's Antiques, 501 Hickory, 915-677-9076

Chapman's, 1117 Pine, 915-672-8563

Crafters Gallery, 2540 Barrow St., 915-695-3257, 100 crafters displays

Elmdale Flea Market, 5423 E. Business 20, 915-673-8623

Gizzmotique, 641 Pecan, 915-677-0041

Historic Hickory Street, 500–700 blocks of Hickory, crafts, antique, and specialty shops in old homes

McCloskey's, 1646 N. 6th, 915-672-6277

One Horse Sleigh, 1009 S. Treadaway, 915-676-1429

R. Honey's, River Oaks Village, 915-698-9696

Red Rooster Collectibles & Flea Market, 1901 S. Treadaway, 915-673-4635

Serendipity, 702 Oak, 915-672-3151

Sharon's Specialties, 721 Hickory, 915-672-1793

Under One Roof, 244 Pine, 915-673-1309, 35 shops

Village Crossing Flea Market, 1505 S. 14, 915-672-5325

Yesterdaze Mall, 2626 E. Hwy 80 (Exit 290), 915-676-9030

Baird, TX, Downtown Antique District, 20 miles east on I-20

Ballinger (915/365-2333) FAX 915-365-3445

Chamber of Commerce, Railroad Avenue and Seventh Street, PO Box 577, Ballinger, TX 76821, E-mail: ballingtx@aol.com; www.ballingertx.org

Population:	4,079
Points of interest:	**Courthouse**
	1909 Carnegie Library is one of thirty-four library buildings funded by Andrew Carnegie and one of only four still in use as a public library.
	Restored Railroad Depot
	Charles H. Noyes Statue, courthouse, sculptured by Pompeo Coppini, dedicated to the "Spirit of the Texas Cowboy."

The Cross, erected by the Jim and Doris Studen Family in 1993

Veterans Memorial on Courthouse Square

Lakes: O. H. Ivie Reservoir twenty miles southeast on FM 1929, east of Hwy 83

Ballinger City Lake, located along historical Elm Creek, features a public swimming pool, playground equipment, picnic area with outdoor cooking facilities, hiking and bike trails, RV hookups, fishing.

Annual events: April: Texas State Festival of Ethnic Cultures and Arts & Crafts Show, held on the "largest landscaped courthouse lawn in the state," features Colorado River Bike Fest, ethnic food booths, handmade arts and crafts, live entertainment, and a dance on Saturday night.

September: Texas State Championship Pinto Bean Cook-off

November: Christmas in Olde Ballinger

Accommodations: Concho Park, Inc, Lake Ivie, 915-357-4466

Desert Inn Motel, Hwy 67 S, 915-365-2518

Elm Creek Village, O. H. Ivie, 915-357-4776

Miz Virginia's Bed & Breakfast, 800-344-0781

Motel Stonewall, 201 Broadway, 915-365-3524, 800-895-7760

Olde Park Hotel, 107 S. 6th, 915-365-2453

Restaurants: Beefmaster Steakhouse, 1608 Broadway, 915-365-2424

China House, Hwy 67 S, 915-365-5627

Dairy Queen, 1200 Hutchins, 915-365-2058

Elm Creek Village, O. H. Ivie, 915-357-4776

Jeweled Sampler, 719 Hutchins, 915-365-5470

Lowake Steakhouse, Lowake, 915-442-3201
Pizza Hut, 204 Broadway, 915-365-2566
Pizza Pro, 610 Hutchins, 915-365-3313
Sonic Drive In, 2003 Hutchins, 915-365-2225
Subway, 1801 Hutchins, 915-365-2876
Taco Paco's, 104 Broadway, 915-365-2226

Specialty
Shopping:

Curiosities, 915-365-5470
The Now & Then Shoppe, 915-365-2653
Olde Park Hotel Complex, 915-365-2453
Stuff N Such, 915-365-5864
The Treadmill, 915-365-3974
Ueckert's Main Street, 915-365-3383
The Woodbox, 915-365-3696

Breckenridge (254/559-2301)

Population:

6,800

Lakes:

Hubbard Creek Lake, Possum Kingdom Lake

Points of interest:

Breckenridge Library and Fine Arts Center, art displays and traveling exhibits. Open Monday–Friday, 11–6, 200 Breckenridge Avenue

Breckenridge Aviation Museum, vintage warplanes, displays and a collection of historic photographs. Open daily from 8–5, at Stephens County Airport, U.S. 183, 2 miles south

Swenson Memorial Museum and J. D. Sandefer Oil Annex, in old bank building, features pioneer artifacts, traveling exhibits. Open Tuesday–Saturday 10–noon, 1–4. Annex is devoted to boom-days history, open-air tool display, oil field history. Located 116 West Walnut and 113 North Breckenridge

Annual events:

January: Stephens County Junior Livestock Show and Sale; Chili Cook-Off

February: Kiwanis Annual Rattlesnake Round-up and Flea Market

April: Stephens Co. Frontier Days

May: Big Bass Bonanza, call for dates; Stephens County Ranch Rodeo

June: KEAN Bass Classic

July: Southern Drag Boat Association Races; Breckenridge Air Show; July 4th Fest

August: Fabulous Fifties Fun Day & Car Show; County Junior Rodeo

November: Craft show

December: Christmas Parade.

Accommodations:

Breckenridge Inn, 3111 W. Walker, 254-559-6502

The Ridge Motel, 2602 W. Walker 254-559-2244

Bakers Bunk House, Hubbard Creek Lake, 254-559-2738

The Blue Rose (B&B) 254-559-2105

Everett Guest House, 254-559-6453

The Keeping Room (B&B) 254-559-8368

Restaurants:

Anchor Drive In

Angels Pizza

Bobby's Burgers

Double M Bar-B-Que

Golden Hut Chinese Restaurant

Ken's Chicken and Fish

Ernie's Spanish Kitchen

L & L Country Cooking

McDonald's

Pam's Cafe

Ridge Restaurant

Sonic Drive-In

Taco Bell

Specialty Shopping:

Angel Art Productions, 103 W. Walker

Antique Shoppe, 105 W. Walker

Antique Depot, 500 E. Walker

Antique Mart, 3114 W. Walker

Wishes, 203 W. Walker

Buffalo Gap (915/572-3347)

Population: 469

Points of interest: **Buffalo Gap Historic Village and Museum**, a complex of twenty historic structures from the former frontier settlement, all restored and furnished, centered around the first county courthouse jail. Exhibits include country store, railroad depot, blacksmith and woodworking shop, nineteenth century doctor-dentist office, two-room school, and 1880 bank, buggies and wagons, firearms and Indian artifacts. Open March 15–November 15, Monday–Saturday, 10–6, Sunday 12–6. Winter hours November 16–March 14, Friday, Saturday 10–5. Sunday 12–5. Admission. 915-572-3365

Abilene State Park (camping), 915-572-3204

Accommodations: Buffalo Gap B&B, 915-572-3145

Restaurants: Bar B Que Barn, Perini Ranch Steakhouse, 915-572-3339

Deutschlander Freshwater Catfish Co., 915-572-3486

Winters (915/754-5210)

Population:	2,899
Points of interest:	Z. I. Hale Museum
	Old buildings on Main Street
	E. V. Spence Reservoir
Annual events:	January: Junior Livestock Show
	May: Mayfest Celebration
	June: Bass Classic
	October: Ranch Heritage Day (Goat Roping Contest and Brisket Cook-off)
	December: Annual Christmas Parade.

During the 1860s Charles Goodnight, Oliver Loving, and others drove large cattle herds to New Mexico and Colorado along the Butterfield Trail, and Indian activity once again became a problem in the region. The Comanches were bellicose, and need of military protection along the upper Concho River country was imperative. Fort Chadbourne, which had more than four hundred troops, provided some security for a period, but it was not located where protection was needed most. Furthermore, the fort continued to suffer from the persistent problem of an inadequate water supply.

Accordingly, in November 1867, an army locating party selected a new site at the junction of the Concho Rivers, where the main (North) branch of the Concho joins the waters of the Middle Concho, Dove Creek, Spring Creek, and South Concho. This location served as the site for construction of a new fort to replace Chadbourne. The post was established in December as Camp

Hatch by 388 men of the Fourth Cavalry under Captain George P. Huntt. The name originated in recognition of Major John P. Hatch of the same regiment. He respectfully declined the honor, and one month later in January it was renamed Camp Kelly in honor of Major Michael J. Kelly, again a member of the Fourth, whose death the previous August inspired the tribute. In February 1868, the post was renamed Fort Concho. (Bitner 1933, 10; Conger 1966, 89, 92; Haley 1952, 126, 130; Gregory 1957, 19)

Fort Concho became at once the focal point of the frontier defense of northwest Texas. As a result of changes in commanders and in plans, it took several years to complete the construction of the post, but once established it remained in use for the next twenty-one years. During that time, the garrison served as regimental headquarters for the Fourth and Tenth Cavalry and the Eleventh and Sixteenth Infantry Regiments. Other units which served at the fort included the Third, Eighth, and Ninth Cavalry and the Seventeenth, Nineteenth, Twenty-Fourth, and Twenty-Fifth Infantry Regiments.

Aside from possessing a substantial source of water, the land around the fort was also capable of providing for the nutritional needs of the military's livestock and mounts. Civilian contractors cut the prairie grass out on the surrounding flatlands from points as far away as forty miles and sold the hay to the military at Fort Concho. Likewise, supplies of mesquite wood and fresh beef were obtained by contract for the post.

By February 1879, the last permanent building—a schoolhouse/chapel—to be constructed at the fort was completed. Civilian craftsmen from the German settlement of Fredericksburg, along with the ample assistance of post personnel, carried out quality masonry construction. By mid-April 1889 approximately thirty-nine buildings, excluding temporary structures, stood on the post grounds. (Bitner 1933, 10; Bell, Klein and Hoffman 1980, 14, 18, 45–51)

During its period of service, the post provided a base of departure for troops participating in some of the primary Indian campaigns carried out in Texas and the surrounding regions during the 1870s. Prior to this, in the first years of the camp's existence, troops engaged in no organized campaigns against the Indians. Like other forts on the western frontier, the troops provided escort and protection for stage lines, cattle herds, wagon trains, and settlers through the territory. This was carried out in conjunction with patrols, scouts, and the continued exploration and mapping of the western plains. (Haley 1952, 149–52)

The Texas frontier in the 1870s provided an ample stage for the campaigns carried out by the foremost of Fort Concho's several noted commanders, Ranald Slidell Mackenzie. His military exploits in Texas are central to the history of the wars against the Southern Plains Indians. A first honor graduate of West Point in 1862, he had received seven brevets in less than three years of combat during the Civil War, and was, at age twenty-six, mustered out of the army in 1866 with the permanent rank of colonel. Mackenzie was considered by some, General Ulysses S. Grant among them, as one of the most promising young officers in the army. (Conger 1966, 93; Wallace 1963, 9–11)

Officers' quarters.

Mackenzie reached Fort Concho on September 6, 1869, with the rank of colonel, in command of the Fourth Cavalry. Described as "imperious and impetuous in manner and design, irritable and irascible on the march, and gallant and invincible in the field," Mackenzie carried the war to the Comanches on the upper Brazos. He and the Fourth Cavalry played an important role in the suppression of Indian resistance in Texas during the 1870s, and it was this regiment which, in September of 1874, engaged in the Battle of Palo Duro Canyon. (Wallace 1963, 138)

One of the most tragic events in Fort Concho's history occurred in the summer of 1877. On August 3, two black troopers rode into Fort Concho to report that Captain Nicholas Nolan and a detachment of black troopers, Company A, Tenth Cavalry, along with a volunteer company of buffalo hunters were lost on the plains and starving for water. Poor judgment, bad management, and indecision by the leaders resulted in the force being scattered in the desert. Some members of the group made it to water in a matter of hours, but one party of soldiers wandered for days, surviving on only the coagulated blood and heavy urine of dying horses. The majority of the expedition's members survived, but four troopers and one civilian perished, along with twenty-three horses and four mules. (Haley 1952, 244–45, 259)

At Fort Concho as at other military centers on the Texas frontier, black troops formed a substantial part of the garrison at various periods in the post's history, and there were occasional clashes between the soldiers and civilians in the community. Such an incident occurred in late January and early February of 1881. Infuriated over the shooting of a black trooper from Company E by local rancher Thomas McCarthy in San Angelo, fellow soldiers formed a mob and entered the small town. The group, said to have ranged in size from thirty to 150 troopers, wounded one man outside a local store and riddled the Nimitz Hotel with bullets after mistakenly believing McCarthy to be inside. Texas Rangers arrived in San Angelo shortly thereafter at the request of the local sheriff. Order was quickly restored after Captain Bryan March of

Headquarters.

the Rangers bluntly warned the post's commander, Colonel Benjamin H. Grierson, that March's men would kill anyone, soldier or otherwise, who crossed the river from the fort and entered San Angelo. On that note, the issue ended. (Haley 1952, 276–82)

One of the more humorous stories to come out of Fort Concho is that of a black soldier named Ellis who was serving with the Tenth Cavalry. Following an illness, he was declared dead by the post doctor. In her article, "The Early History of the Concho Country and Tom Green County," Grace Bitner offers a colorful account of the story of "Dead" Ellis:

No account of Fort Concho is complete without the story of "Dead" Ellis who "died" in the hospital about nine o'clock one morning. He was laid out on the "cooling board" and put in the dead house, a room connected with the laundry of the hospital. That night four negroes, including "Old" Cox who tells the story, went to the dead house to sit up with the body. Cox explains that they had a pot of coffee and two jugs of whiskey, and before long were feeling pretty happy. About eleven o'clock one of the men went to the door of the dead house to look at the corpse. Ellis's hands and feet had been tied. Just as the man looked in, the corpse began to wiggle. The negro yelled, "That man ain't dead; he's movin', he's gettin' up." Needless to say, some other negroes were moving also. Three made a dash for the door at once and all got jammed in so that none could get out. Cox jumped through the window, shutter and all, followed closely by another which he thought to be "Dead Ellis for sure." Ellis was returned to the hospital where he recovered from illness and was able to report back to duty within a matter of days. (Bitner 1933, 12–13)

Fort Concho was abandoned as a military post in June 1889. Restoration of the post, now designated as a National Historic Landmark, began in 1929. The garrison also has the distinction of being the best preserved western frontier fort in the United States. The interesting part of Concho's preservation has been the fact that it has been preserved through the efforts of the citizens of San Angelo.

The people of San Angelo have also restored other historic sites in their community, including the historic area on downtown Concho Street. One of the more famous buildings is Miss Hattie's Museum, a restored "ladies of the evening saloon and parlor house."

Two communities grew up around Fort Concho: Ben Ficklin and Santa Angela. Ben Ficklin was a small settlement and stage coach stand four miles south of San Angelo. People settled around the stage station, and in 1875 Ben Ficklin became the county seat of Tom Green County. Unfortunately for the community, it was washed away by a flood in 1882, and the people and the county seat moved to San Angelo.

Santa Angela was established by Bartholomew J. DeWhitt in 1868 across the river from the fort. At first it consisted of only a saloon and a couple of gambling halls and was known as "Over the River." As time passed and the community grew, it was deemed that the town needed a better name. Consequently it was named for Mrs. DeWhitt's sister who was the Mother Superior of Ursuline Convent in San Antonio, Santa Angela. It was shortened to San Angela and that name was later changed as the United States government objected to a post office having a masculine "San" and a feminine "Angela," so it became San Angelo.

San Angelo prospered on sheep, goats, and cattle during the early days and oil in the twentieth century. San Angelo is known as the mohair capitol of the world and is the primary wool market in the United States. It is also the home of Angelo State University.

From San Angelo, head south along U. S. Highway 277 which will lead to Christoval. The Twin Buttes may be seen on the right, now marking Twin Butte Reservoir. The upper road from San Antonio to El Paso merged in this vicinity with east-west travel.

Alternate Route: When leaving Christoval you may wish to continue south along U. S. Highway 277 to Sonora to visit the Caverns and then take County Road 864 to Fort McKavett.

From Christoval head southeast along FM 2084 that leads into Schleicher County.

Continue along 2084 until you reach U. S. Highway 190, then turn east to County Road 864 which will take you to Fort McKavett.

The highway runs close to the South Concho River, the region to which R. F. Tankersley brought his herd of seven hundred cattle in 1864. To the west of this highway some eight miles, and sixteen miles southwest of San Angelo, the Battle of Dove Creek was fought between approximately 350 minutemen and Confederate troops and a large force of Kickapoo Indians, skirting the frontier on their way to Mexico with their families. The attack by the troops was a costly failure. They were beaten off, with twenty-two men killed and eighteen wounded.

Christoval, renowned for its clear water and shade trees, was quite a health spa during the early part of the twentieth century. Although it did not rival Mineral Wells, people traveled many miles to take the waters of Christoval. Many churches had encampments in the community and held their retreats in Christoval. Today a couple of the old bath houses still stand, but as one old-timer said, the "hot tub" put them out of business.

Schleicher County was created in 1877 and named in honor of Gustav Schleicher, a German-American engineer, soldier, and statesman. In 1876 a New Yorker, William L. Black, purchased thirty thousand acres for ten cents an acre at the headspring of the San Saba River. The area was opened to settlement when a well drilled in 1872 demonstrated that underground water could be had in this region even though surface water was not available over great stretches of the land.

TOURIST INFORMATION
(When possible please call ahead to be sure these services are still available.)

Fort Concho (915/481-2646/657-4444)

Points of interest: **Twenty-three original and restored fort structures** (National Historic Landmark). Authentically refurbished exhibit buildings include a restored headquarters, soldiers barracks, officer's quarters, chapel/school, and post hospital. Exhibits tell the story of the fort, the Indian campaigns and of San Angelo. Open Tuesday–Saturday, 10–5, Sunday 1–5. Closed Thanksgiving, Christmas and New Years. Call the Chamber of Commerce for the dates of Christmas at Fort Concho.

Four living history units: Fort Concho Infantry, Sixteenth Regiment, Co. F, (ca. 1880); Fort Concho Cavalry, Fourth Regiment, Co. D, (ca. 1872); Fort Concho Buffalo Soldiers, Tenth Regiment, Co. D, (ca. 1878), who also travel to perform in other communities

Museum and bookstore

San Angelo (800-375-1206/915-653-1206)

Population: 87,980

Lakes and rivers: Lake Nasworthy and the Concho River Walk

University: Angelo State University

Points of interest: **Concho River pearls**, formed in freshwater mussels, pearls range in color from pink to rich purple. Local jewelers offer a large variety of unique settings for these rare pearls from the lakes and rivers around San Angelo.

Concho River Walk, located downtown, has over six miles of jogging/walking trails, with flowing fountains and water treatments, outdoor stage, small amusement park, nine-hole golf course.

Concho Street, El Paseo de Santa Angela, across Concho River from Fort Concho, is a street that hosted off-duty soldiers from the fort. This historic district features antique shops, saddle shops, cafes.

Museum of Fine Arts, contains changing exhibits of different media from many eras. Open Tuesday–Saturday 10–4. Fort Concho quartermaster building at Burgess Street and Avenue G.

E. H. Danner Museum of Telephony contains models of telephones from Alexander Graham Bell's Gallows Frame Phone (only five were ever built) through wooden phones and push-button phones of the 1880s to present day models. Open museum hours in Officer's Quarters No. 4.

Miss Hattie's Bordello Museum, upstairs at 18 East Concho, is a restored "ladies of the evening" saloon parlor that was a surreptitious San Angelo landmark for decades. Faithfully restored with original furnishing and fashions to depict the living style of those who entertained soldiers, ranchers and cowboys. The house operated from the mid 1800's until closed by the Texas Rangers in 1946. The museum is open Tuesday–Saturday, 9:30–4.

Robert Wood Johnson Museum of Frontier Medicine contains instruments, medicines, surgical kits, hospital furniture, and other items of a typical nineteenth century frontier hospital, some on loan from Johnson & Johnson collection. Also contains items related to San Angelo's medical history. Located in North Ward of the Post Hospital.

Old Chicken Farm Art Center

San Angelo Nature Center, located in the former Lake Rangers Headquarters building at Lake Nasworthy, built by Works Progress Administration. Natural science and history museum emphasizing understanding of Edwards Plateau region. Displays feature native wildlife, live reptiles and amphibians, mounted birds and other wildlife, 200 gallon aquarium, glass enclosed beehive and ant farm. Audiovisual programs. In Mary Lee Park on Knickerbocker at Lake Nasworthy.

Cactus Hotel

Angelo State University Planetarium, the nation's fourth largest university planetarium, features a three dimensional view of the universe. Open when classes are in session, Thursday 8 PM and Saturday 2 PM, in Nursing-Physical Science Building on campus.

Pictographs of Paint Rock

Annual events: Fort Concho and San Angelo

March: San Angelo Stock Show & Rodeo; Fort Concho Equestrian Review

April: Texas Wine Festival; Fort Concho Equestrian Review

May: Full Riding Fiesta

June: World Championship Goat Roping; Wild West Ballonfest; Juneteenth

July 4: Fiesta Del Concho; Pops Concert

September: Fiestas Patrias

October: Octoberfest

November: Steer and Calf Roping Fiesta

December: Christmas at Old Fort Concho

Accommodations: The Hinkle Haus B&B, 19 S. Park Street, 915-653-1931

Julia Wermer B&B, 438 W. Twohig, 915-659-1027

River Inn B&B, 305 W. Twohig, 915-658-9747

Contact Chamber of Commerce or Yellow Pages for listings of major chains.

Restaurants: Cactus Coffee & Tea, 36 E. Twohig, 915-659-1470

Concho Pearl/Raphael Tuck's English Pub, 2400 College Hills Blvd., 915-655-0967

Fuentes Original Cafe, 9 E. Ave. K, 915-658-4081

Old Time Pit Bar-B-Q, 915-655-2771

Contact Chamber of Commerce or Yellow Pages for complete listings

Specialty Shopping: American British Antiques, 87 South, 915-658-6541

Arc Light Antiques, 230 S. Chadbourne, 915-653-8832

Concho Confetti, 42 E. Concho, 915-655-3962

Dee's Centerpiece, Airport Lobby, 915-944-1221

Eggemeyers's General Store, 35 E. Concho, 915-655-1166

Fiesta! Dolls & Collectibles, 226 S. Oakes, 915-658-4023

Jewel of the Concho, 10 E. Concho, 915-653-8782

Miss Hattie's, 18 E. Concho, 915-655-2518

Needful Things, 20 E. Concho, 915-659-6930

Sonora (915/387-2880)

Population:	2,924
Points of interest:	**Caverns of Sonora** contain formations in delicate crystal beauty and amazing profusion on ceilings, walls, and floors. Guided cave tours regularly each half hour covers about 1.5 miles underground. Rest stops are provided, but the tours are strenuous, equivalent to climbing several hundred steps. West of Sonora about eight miles, exit I-10 on Caverns of Sonora Road (FM 1989). Camping area with hookups are available. Admission.

Miers Home Museum

Santa Fe Depot

Main Street

Sutton County Heritage Square

Covered Wagon Outdoor Dinner Theatre, 915-387-2381, performed in a small, natural amphitheater near the Caverns of Sonora. Costumed storytellers recall the early days of the area along with a variety of musical entertaiment. Usually mid June through mid August. Call chamber of commerce for information. Admission.

Annual events:

January: Sutton County Stock Show

March: Ram Test Field Day/Sale

April: West Texas Championship Bar-B-Que & Chili Cook Off

May: Cinco de Mayo Celebration; Sonora Sensation (Calf, Team & Steer Roping)

June: Sonora Wool Show & National Judging Contest; Covered Wagon Dinner Theatre

July: Angora Goat Show & Sale

August: Sutton County Days & Outlaw Pro-Rodeo
September: Diez y Seis de Septiembre Celebrations
October: Ride from the Border Bike Tour
November: Annual Sutton County Game Dinner &
    Hunters Ball

Accommodations: Devils River Inn, 915-387-3516
Holiday Host Motel, 915-387-2531
Twin Oaks Motel, 915-387-2551
Zola's Courts, 915-387-3000

Restaurants: Big Tree Restaurant, 915-387-9923
La Mexicana, 915-387-3401
Rosie's Cafe, 915-387-5552
Sutton County Steak House, 915-387-3833

Construction began on Fort McKavett during the summer of 1852, another in a line of new forts established to protect the westward advance of settlers and travelers through central Texas. The post received its name in honor of Captain Henry McKavett, an officer killed on September 21, 1846, during the Battle of Monterrey while serving with the Eighth Infantry during the Mexican War. (Sullivan 1969, 138) Five companies of this same regiment, under the command of Colonel Thomas Staniford, arrived on the banks of the San Saba River in March 1852. Orders issued by General Persifer Smith, military commander in Texas, specified the new post location at the headspring of the San Saba. This was initially adhered to, though by May a more suitable site was chosen approximately two miles downriver which afforded a natural spring and lagoon.

The post was constructed roughly three hundred yards from the lagoon and five hundred yards from the river, providing the

fort with an unending supply of water. (Sullivan 1969; Crimmins 1950, 308)

By the following August, Colonel W. G. Freeman, making an official inspection, reported that five companies of the Eighth Infantry, numbering 192 officers and enlisted men, were on station at Fort McKavett. They were under the command of Lieutenant Colonel Edmund Brooke Alexander, an 1823 graduate of West Point. Freeman's report noted that the post was still under construction, and that the regiment's officers were living in "small stone buildings of one room designed as kitchens to the quarters proposed to be put up." The report on Fort McKavett also stated that enlisted quarters "are five stone blocks, each eighty by twenty feet, which would be very comfortable if they were finished, but they now require flooring, windows, doors and kitchens." Freeman pointed out that locally there was an abundance of stone for masonry work as well as oak and pecan for basic rough construction, though for some of the above mentioned items "lumber of a better description ought to be furnished."

Regarding the troops posted to the fort, the colonel observed a variety of arms and clothing in use including outdated muskets and uniforms. This problem was of concern, though deficiencies in materials and equipment were characteristic of most frontier forts at this time. Freeman did make special note of Company F, a mounted unit. Such units were not used as extensively prior to the Civil War as they would be in later frontier defense. Freeman wrote on this particular occasion that the ninety-six-man company had available only "30 serviceable and 7 unserviceable horses; but it is wretchedly equipped, being deficient in many essential articles and without the means of keeping in order those at hand." He stated that he was in complete agreement with the possibility of the company being dismounted: "For it is now everywhere conceded that the experiment of mounting infantry has not been successful." (Crimmins 1950, 312)

During the 1850s three regiments received postings to Fort McKavett: the Eighth Infantry, the Second Dragoon Regiment, and the First Infantry. Two companies of this latter regiment were on station at the fort in July 1856 when Colonel J. K. F. Mansfield conducted a second inspection. The post was at this time occupied by 168 troops consisting of five officers, 162 enlisted men, and one assistant surgeon under the command of Lieutenant Colonel H. Bainbridge. (Crimmins 1939, 361, 364–65)

In contrast to the inspection report of 1853, Colonel Mansfield observed that the post was now well armed and clothed and commented approvingly on all aspects of general maintenance, from books and records, to camp discipline and the quality of living conditions at the post. He stated in his report that Fort McKavett was "undoubtedly an important post in the chain [of forts] and should be maintained." (Cummins 1939, 361, 364)

During the course of its occupation, the living and health conditions at McKavett necessarily fluctuated. As was the case in other frontier posts there was, from time to time, considerable illness among the fort's occupants. With a mean strength of 225 men, in the course of one year—ending on June 30, 1853—1,043 cases of disease were recorded. Nearly half of these cases were diagnosed as "intermittent fever," a generic term which doctors today say might have included malaria and half a dozen other ailments. Of the remaining cases reported, one hundred and eighty-four were diseases of organs associated with the digestive system, and fifty-three were pulmonary in nature. (Crimmins 1950, 313) Tarantula bites proved serious for several men. Colonel Freeman reported that the post gardens were excellent, and he volunteered information that in early spring before most vegetables are in season, servings of poke salad and wild lamb lettuce kept down scurvy. (Crimmins 1950, 315)

Disease remained a constant element to contend with on the frontier, and Fort McKavett was never immune. It did however maintain a traditionally low record of disease in later years. Despite a relatively heavy number of illnesses at the post in 1873, including cases of typhoid fever, the Surgeon General's office stated that the location and natural environment of the fort and its vicinity "have all combined to give this post and its locality the name of being exceeding healthy." (War Department 1875, 217, 219)

Indian activity in the region was not heavy during the 1850s, though a brief rise in hostile raids in the spring of 1854 and continued activity into 1855, occupied the post's companies. Comanche chiefs Buffalo Hump, Sanaco, Ketumseh, and Yellow

Officers' quarters.

Wolf frequently honored the post with a visit, but Comanches caused less trouble here than at Fort Chadbourne during the 1850s. Military patrols and scouting parties were regularly deployed in the field to monitor Indian activity in the region between the Llano and Concho Rivers. In later years of the decade, hostile Indian activity in north Texas demanded a corresponding redeployment of troops northward. This shift resulted in the closure of Fort McKavett in 1859. (Sullivan 1969, 141)

Reactivation of the post did not occur until 1868. One company of the Fourth Cavalry under the command of Lieutenant Colonel Eugene B. Beaumont reestablished the post on March 30. The post had fallen into considerable decay during the preceding decade. According to Surgeon N. D. Middleton, "The post was found to be one mass of ruins, only one house was habitable, and the whole command was forced to go under canvas." Reconstruction began immediately. (Sullivan 1969, 143)

Following its reoccupation, an assortment of regimental companies were posted to McKavett in the years following the Civil

Hospital and Interpretive Center.

War. These included elements of the First, Tenth, Sixteenth, and Twenty-Second Infantry Regiments, as well as four black regiments: the Ninth and Tenth Cavalry and the Twenty-Fourth and Twenty-Fifth Infantry. Of the latter, the Twenty-Fourth was actually organized at Fort McKavett from portions of the Thirty-Eighth and Forty-First Infantry. Restoration of the post's facilities were still under way on March 15, 1869, when Colonel Ranald S. Mackenzie arrived to take command of the Twenty-Fourth. Troops from McKavett spent much time in patrolling the region against marauders and shared in every major campaign on the Texas frontier in the 1870s. (Sullivan 1969)

During Mackenzie's short tenure at Fort McKavett, two incidents occurred which involved both the military and the private citizens from the surrounding area. The first began in March 1869, when Mackenzie placed a contingent of troops at Kickapoo Springs, twenty-five miles north of the fort, at the request of Ben Ficklin, the renowned mail and stage superintendent. Ficklin wanted a permanent military post there, but Mackenzie insisted that the troops were not available for such an undertaking and recalled the detachment two months later. Ficklin did persuade higher military authorities to order the troops returned to Kickapoo Springs while Mackenzie was temporarily away from his command. This produced a sharp protest to headquarters from Mackenzie upon his return, but the troops remained there for some time, however, not in any permanent capacity. (Sullivan 1969, 145–46)

The second event was characterized by excitement and tension which plagued the post and community of Fort McKavett that same summer. John M. "Humpy" Jackson, a prominent white farmer of the vicinity, shot and killed a black trooper because a second black soldier had written a note of endearment to Jackson's daughter. A two-year hunt for Jackson by the military resulted before he finally surrendered to authorities in the fall of 1871. In the end, a sympathetic jury cleared him of all charges in a state court. (Sullivan 1969, 144)

When not on campaign, the fort's primary activities centered on routine patrols, scouts, and escort duties throughout their designated region. Indian activity in the general vicinity of the post slackened during the latter half of the 1870s, and consequently the fort's importance as a frontier post declined. In 1882 the main complement of troops moved out of Fort McKavett for redeployment, leaving only Company D, Sixteenth Infantry to occupy the fort. In June 1883, this final detachment abandoned the post. (Sullivan 1969, 148–49)

Today, Fort McKavett is designated by the state of Texas as a State Historic Site.

Leaving Fort McKavett, head east along 864 until you once again reach Highway 190. Then continue east to Menard.

The county seat of Menard County, both Menard and the county were named for Michael B. Menard who had been involved in the founding of Galveston. Colonel Menard was primarily responsible for keeping the Indian tribes on the frontier at peace during the Texas Revolution. The county was created in 1858 and organized in 1871. The townsite of Menard, then called Menardville, was laid out the same year. The town was a stop for the cattle drovers heading north or west, and quite often the old Spanish Mission just west of town served as a holding corral. Cattle, sheep, and goats have long been the fortune of the community. It was the Spaniards that began the recorded history of the area when they established the San Saba Presidio, called Presidio San Luis de Amarillas, in 1757. Its purpose was to guard the Mission San Saba de la Santa Cruz down the river a few miles, and also to protect a settlement of some two hundred people. The mission was established for the benefit of the Apache Indians of this vicinity, but the Apaches never found a convenient reason to stay at the mission and be converted. The mission and presidio, located in the country the Comanches also claimed, antagonized the Comanches who were enemies of the Apaches and, therefore, enemies of any friends of the Apaches. The Comanches and their Indian allies, the Nortefios (Wichitas and other Indians of the north) came in 1758, destroyed the mission, and killed most of its occupants.

The presidio held out against the Comanches and in 1759, stout-hearted Diego Ortiz Parrilla, who had held high offices on both sides of the Atlantic under his king, led five hundred troops and Indians into north Texas, striking the Red River at Spanish Fort in Montague County where the Wichitas (Taovayas) had a fort, and the Comanches were standing by. The Indians administered a humiliating defeat to the Spaniards. The mission was not rebuilt. The Presidio of San Saba held on against repeated flailings by the Comanches until 1768, when the remaining Spanish families were removed and the fort abandoned. Today there is a golf course laid out around the ruins.

During their tenure in the area the Spaniards were excited over reports of gold and silver in the Menard country, and they continued to search for La Mina de las Amarillas and La Mina de los Almagres reputed to be located in the region. There are numerous stories of the vast amount of silver supposedly extracted from the mines by the priests, but no one has ever found it—except, perhaps, James Bowie.

Stories abound about Bowie making friends with Chief Xolic of the Lipan Apaches who showed up in San Antonio twice a year to barter for goods. He always had small amounts of silver. Bowie supposedly lived with the Lipans for a period of time and became one of them. They in turn showed him where the mines were. Whether the story is true or not history has not said. We do know that on November 2, 1831, James and his brother Rezin set out from San Antonio in search of the mines. On the nineteenth Bowie was warned by friendly Comanches that hostile Indians were in the neighborhood. On the morning of the twenty-first, 164 hostiles attacked Bowie's band of eleven. Caught somewhat by surprise, Bowie's group did have the protection of a thicket and nearby Calf Creek. The fight lasted all day, and the Indians found the small band to be more than they had anticipated. The Indians lost fifty and had thirty-five wounded, while Bowie lost one and had three wounded. The Indians decided they would do battle another day. The site became known as Bowie's Fort, and, according to Rezin, the mine was not far from where the battle took place. Previously, Rezin had been in the cave, and with his tomahawk had hacked off some ore and taken it to New Orleans. The assayer's report at that time had proven it to be a rich claim, but before James could exploit the mine, the Texas Revolution began. Thus Bowie's mine joins the other legendary mines that occasionally sends prospectors into the hills around Menard. (Pierce 1946, 31–39)

Ruins of officers' quarters.

TOURIST INFORMATION

(When possible please call ahead to be sure these services are still available.)

Fort McKavett State Historic Site

(915-396-2358) P.O. Box 867, Fort McKavett, TX 76841

Open daily 8–5

Population:	103
Points of Interest:	Currently, **fifteen buildings have been restored**, including officers' quarters, hospital barracks, post headquarters, school house, bakery, dead house, sink, and ruins of numerous others.
	Interpretive exhibits in the old hospital ward trace the history of the Fort McKavett area, emphasizing military history, the post-military community, and historic archeaology.
	A self-guided trail leads to the military lime kiln and "Government Springs."
	Picnic tables are available for day use.
Annual Events:	March: Annual Re-enactment; Weapons demonstration upon request

Menard

Population:	1,774
Points of interest:	**Ruins of Real Presidio de San Sabá**, Spanish fort established in 1751 to protect Mission Santa Cruz de San Sabá. Ruins maintained as county park two miles west off Texas 29. Picnic facilities and adjacent campgrounds.
	Menard County Museum, 100 Frisco Avenue, contains local history exhibits and frontier artifacts

housed in small, vintage railroad depot. Open Monday–Wednesday 9–5. Admission.

Historic Ditch Walk, which features remnants of the old irrigation ditch built by the Spanish in the mid-1750s, several early churches, the Pioneer Rest Cemetery, the San Saba Presidio, and Fort McKavett State Historical Park.

Country Store contains locally produced handicrafts, arts and foods.

Annual Events:

September: Jim Bowie days
October: Silver Mine Classic Lamb Show

FORT
Mason

*Upon leaving Menard head east along Texas Highway 29 to **Fort Mason**, located on a hill south of **Mason**.*

Mason grew up around the fort and became the county seat in 1861. Mason County was created on January 22, and organized on August 2, 1858. It is said that the first settlers who drifted into the region in 1846 were from John 0. Meusebach's settlement in Fredericksburg. Because the settlers were beyond the protection of government troops, Meusebach negotiated a treaty with the Comanches to allow his settlers to live in peace. Unfortunately the peace did not last, and the settlers were soon demanding protection.

Fortunately, the United States Army was already developing a plan to establish a chain of forts to provide protection across the Texas frontier. During the 1850s, as settlers began to

move into central Texas, an ever-increasing need arose for armed protection against Indian attacks in the region. To this end, the United States army established the forts at approximately fifty-mile intervals to provide a network of defense for the civilian communities. Fort Mason was one of the posts which provided this service.

German colonists who located in Fredericksburg and the surrounding vicinity in the 1840s succeeded initially in making a treaty of peace with Comanches in the region, but a resurgence in Indian activity soon forced them to call on Washington to provide increased military protection.

During its nineteen years of service from 1851 to 1869, Fort Mason alternated between periods of military activation and deactivation. (Simpson 1966, 142) Beginning in the spring of 1851 Major William J. Hardee, leading approximately two hundred troops of the Second Dragoons from Fort Martin Scott near Fredericksburg—Fort Scott was established in December 1848—began scouting for a suitable location to construct a post to the north, between the Pedernales and Colorado Rivers. The post was established in July 1851 by Brevet Major H. W. Merrill and Companies A (from Fort Croghan) and B (from Fort Martin Scott) of the Second Dragoons. (Bierschwale 1968, 8–9)

Though the origin of the fort's name is uncertain, it is believed to have originated in honor of Second Lieutenant George T. Mason, killed on April 25, 1846, during the skirmish which precipitated the Mexican War. Lieutenant Mason, as part of a scouting force of United States Dragoons, engaged a larger force of Mexican cavalry at Rancho Carricitos near La Rosia. In the ensuing battle the entire detachment of dragoons was either killed or captured. Being an accomplished swordsman, Lieutenant Mason chose to continue to fight rather than surrender his weapon, and was killed. (Simpson 1966, 143; Bierschwale 1968, 8–9)

With the assistance of civilian masons and carpenters Merrill and his troops constructed the fort, drawing extensively on the native red sandstone and timber found in the surrounding area. When completed, the post was capable of providing adequate facilities for the care of a full regiment, though it appears that a force of no more than two hundred men was ever stationed at the fort at any one time.

For troops stationed at Fort Mason a relatively comfortable environment existed. The fort was situated atop Post Hill, which commanded a panoramic view of the countryside to the north. In her diary, Mrs. Albert Sidney Johnston wrote that "the view from the fort is one of the most extensive that I have ever seen." (Simpson 1968, 143)

The quality of living conditions at the post is perhaps best reflected in the following excerpts taken from a report made by Colonel W. G. Freeman, who inspected Fort Mason on August 15, 1853.

> The site is elevated and salubrious, commanding an extensive view of the surrounding country, stone and lime are procured in abundance in the immediate vicinity, and an unfailing supply of pure spring water is found within 400 yards. . . . The buildings were constructed entirely by the command and are substantial and comfortable. . . .

The company quarters were neat and well ventilated; the provisions of the men were wholesome and well cooked, and the messing arrangements, generally, excellent. There is a fine garden which contributes much to the comfort of the command. I was particularly pleased to find each company provided with a small library of standard works. (Crimmins 1950, 204, 206)

Even though the post maintained a reputation as one of the finest in the Department of Texas, it was closed in January 1854. For the next two years the post remained unoccupied, and the state of defense on this frontier deteriorated. The following year, in January 1856, the United States Second Cavalry Regiment reoccupied the post, and conditions rapidly improved in the region. Colonel Albert Sidney Johnston commanded the regiment, and Lieutenant Colonel Robert E. Lee was second in authority. Among the other officers posted to the fort at this time were Major George H. Thomas and Captain Edmund Kirby Smith.

From this location contingents of the Second Cavalry scouted the country almost continuously. "All companies have killed Indians except Captain Stoneman's," wrote an officer from the fort in 1857. Continued Indian activity no doubt provided Stoneman's company an opportunity to rectify this record. One scout, Lieutenant John Bell Hood, destined to later command a Confederate army, was drawn into an Indian ambush on the Devil's River. In this encounter the Comanches, displaying a white flag, baited the soldiers into the trap. During the skirmish, in which the Indians set fire to the surrounding grassland, two troopers were killed and several wounded.

Following the brief abandonment of the post in early 1859 a pronounced increase in Indian marauding again developed. The return of elements of the Second Cavalry, under Captains Earl

Officer's quarters.

Van Dorn and Richard W. Johnson, soon suppressed this activity and conditions once again improved.

During periods of the fort's military occupation the complement of troops stationed there fluctuated. Of particular importance to the overall character of the fort were the soldiers themselves. The following data from the census of 1860, concerning the enlisted men at Fort Mason, provides insight into the ethnic heritage of the troops posted there. The country of birth of 118 of the men is as follows: Ireland, 43; south of the Mason-Dixon Line other than Texas, 22; north of the Mason-Dixon Line, 19; Germany, 18; British Isles other than Ireland, 7; Texas, 3. France, Mexico, and Denmark were also represented.

Though Fort Mason was on the western frontier it was not unaffected by the events which developed in the eastern United States in 1861. While commanding the Second Cavalry and Fort Mason early that same year, Robert E. Lee experienced a great deal of ambivalence as a result of the disunion movement then under way. Both his native state of Virginia and the American Union were very dear to him and he was, at this time, torn by his personal loyalties. Following the reception of official orders to report to Washington, Lee relinquished command of his regiment on February 13, and returned to Virginia. The following spring he resigned from the United States Army, and ultimately achieved the distinction as the most revered Confederate general in Civil War history.

The Confederate States Army assumed control of Fort Mason in March 1861. It was used only periodically during the war years, although the site did have the distinction of serving for a short time as a prison camp for Union prisoners. Such conditions were not destined to last, and, with the defeat of the Confederacy in 1865, control of the site eventually reverted back to the United States Army. On December 24, 1866, it was reoccupied by the Fourth United States Cavalry. One month later the post, now serving as the headquarters of that regiment, housed a sizable force of 445 soldiers and 330 serviceable horses. (Bierschwale 1968, 34)

As the fort grew, it played a significant role in the development of the neighboring community of Mason. Settlers came into Mason County from Fredericksburg and the surrounding area as

early as 1846. The county was organized in 1858 with the town of Mason, situated just north of the fort, serving as the county seat. Though a good rapport did exist between Fort Mason and the growing settlement the relationship was not without incident. In November 1867, Major John A. Thompson and Sergeant John McDougal were killed while trying to quell a row in a local saloon between a number of troops and townspeople.

Listed in the last inspection of the post on January 13, 1869, were twenty-five buildings occupied by a single company of sixty-nine men. One month later on March 23, 1869, Fort Mason was closed.

A substantial number of officers assigned to this post during the pre-Civil War period from 1851 to 1861 went on to become distinguished military generals. Aside from the names already mentioned as having served at Fort Mason, other well-known figures include William J. Hardee and Fitzhugh Lee, Confederate States Army; and Philip St. George Cooke, United States Army.

Little remains of Fort Mason today. Following its closure in 1869 much of the post was dismantled by local settlers and townspeople who used the materials in the construction of numerous local homes and businesses. Only the remains of the post's cavalry stable can still be seen. A reconstruction of one of the officer's

quarters, situated on original foundations, was completed in 1976 under the direction of the late Kurt Qzesch. The structure stands on Post Hill, approximately five blocks south of Mason's town square.

The people of Mason, conscious of their historical past, have worked hard to preserve the frontier flavor of their community. On the Mason National Register Historic District list there are approximately fifty commercial and residential structures. The town square is a major part of that historic district and is dominated by the courthouse which was built in 1909. The community has a German atmosphere similar to Fredericksburg, especially in the area of cuisine and merchandise. Another interesting attraction near Mason is the Mason Bat Cave, located in the James River area, sixteen miles south. It is said to shelter a bat population estimated to rival that of Carlsbad Caverns.

Trooper 1854-1858

TOURIST INFORMATION

(When possible please call ahead to be sure these services are still available.)

Fort Mason

Reconstruction of the officer's quarters stands atop Post Hill, which can be reached from downtown via Post Hill Street. A number of crumbling foundations still show some sites of 23 original buildings that included barracks, officers' quarters, storehouses, stables, guardhouse and hospital. The reconstructed building is on original foundations; double fireplace foundations are original, and rock used was from original building materials of fort.

Mason

(915/347-5758)

Chamber of Commerce, 108 Ft. McKavett, Mason, TX 76856

Population:	2,100
Points of interest:	**Greek Revival courthouse**
	Seaquist Victorian Mansion, 400 Broad Street, built of sandstone, the 22-room house is elaborately detailed with carved limestone. Group tours are available by calling 512-352-6415.
	Eckert James River Bat Cave Preserve, open from May–October, Thursday–Sunday, 6–9, you can visit one of the largest Mexican free-tailed bat colonies known. Call 915-347-5970 for information and directions.
	Mason County Memorial Museum
	Mason County M. Beven Eckert Memorial Library contains an exhibit detailing career of author of *Old Yeller* and other works, Fred Gibson.
	Topaz hunting, write or call Wesley Loeffler, Menard Route, Mason, Texas 76856, 915-347-6415, or stop

at Nu-Way Grocery on the northwest corner of the square. Country Collectibles on U.S. 87 North, Benji's Books and Gifts, and Underwood's Antiques on the square offer cut and mounted stones. **Gene Zesch's Woodcarving exhibit**, Commercial Bank

Annual events: January: Mason County Jr. Livestock Show
April: Bluebonnet Country Lanes Drives; Home Tour
May: Wildflower Country Lanes Drives; Mother's Day Craft Show
June: Open Tennis Tournament; Catfish Fry
July: Roundup Rodeo and Parade; Arts and Crafts Show
September: Tejano Festival
October: Fall Festival; Over the Hill Tennis Tournament
November: Christmas Lighting Tours; Wild Game Dinner; Craft Show
December: Christmas Lighting Tour; Home Tour

Accommodations: The Bridge's House B&B, 800-776-3519; 915-347-6440
Carriage House, Westmoreland Street, 915-347-6829 or 347-5589
Cottage on Live Oak Street, 915-347-5531
Das Altes Haus, 4 miles NE of Mason on Old Pontotoc Road, 915-347-5719
The Hasse House, Hwy 29 East, Art, Texas, 915-347-6463
Hill Country Inn, Hwy 87 N, 915-347-6317
The Martin Guest Ranch, Hwy 87 S/RR 1723, 915-347-6852

Mason Square Bed & Breakfast, north side of the Square, 800-369-0405, 915-347-6398

Mi Casa es Su Casa, 1117 El Paso Street, 915-347-5342

Old Liberty B&B, Hwy 87 S, 915-347-6685

Oma's and Opa's Haus, 510 El Paso Street, 800-508-5101, 915-347-6477

Pontotoc Ranch B & B, Hickory Grove Rd., 915-251-6630

RV Park, Fort Mason City Park, Hwy 87 S, 915-347-6449

Smith I Bar Ranch, 915-265-4272 or 210-826-2800

Willow Creek Ranch, 14 miles South of Mason, 915-347-6781, FAX 888-281-7242, E-mail: willowcr@hctc.net

Restaurants:

The Bistro, on the Square

Cooper's Pit BBQ, Hwy 87 S, 915-347-6897

The Coffee Shop, on the Square, 915-347-6398

Dairy Queen, Hwy 87 N, 915-347-5905

Fred's Steakhouse, Hwy 87 N, 915-347-5876

Friendly Cafe, Hwy 87 N, 347-6435

Willow Creek Cafe, on the Square, 915-347-6124

Zavala's Restaurant, Hwy 87 N, 915-347-5365

Specialty Shopping:

Antiques & Crafts, on the Square, 915-347-6440

Antique Emporium, on the Square, 915-347-5330

Benji's Books & gifts, on the Square, 915-347-6323

County Collectibles, on Hwy 87 N, 915-347-5249

Hinckley's Country Store, on the Square, 915-347-6824

Hodgepodge, on the Square

Hoffman Dry Goods Co., on the Square, 915-347-6750

Lindas's Boutique, on the Square, 915-347-5553

Market Square, on the Square, 915-347-5516

P. V.'s Antiques, on the Square, 915-347-5516

Ramona's Gallery of Art, on the Square, 915-347-6635

Underwood Antique Mall, on the Square, 915-347-5258

R. W. Zgabay Clothiers, on the Square, 915-347-6896

Fredericksburg

(210-997-6523)

106 N. Adams, Fredericksburg, TX 78624. FAX 997-8588.

E-mail asstdir@ktc.com

Home Page Address: http:www.fredericksburg-texas.com/

Settled by German immigrant families in 1846, many older buildings retain traditional German styles. German is still spoken occasionally, and old customs are regularly observed: Easter Fires, Schuetzenfests (marksmanship tournaments), Oktoberfest, Kristkindl Markt, and Kinderfest.

Population:	7,500
Points of interest:	**Admiral Nimitz Museum and Historical Center**, 210-997-4379, 340 E. Main Street. The Steamboat Hotel structure, originally built in 1852, contains three floors of the Museum of the Pacific War, dedicated to everyone who served in the Pacific under Admiral Nimitz. Features of the building include the ballroom, and four original refurnished guest rooms. The Japanese Garden of Peace is a gift from the people of Japan. The History Walk of the Pacific War, located a block from the garden, displays guns,

planes, boats, tanks, etc. Nimitz Museum Bookstore. Open 8–5 daily. Admission.

Bauer Toy Museum, 210-997-9394, 233 E. Main. Open 1–4:30 weekdays and Sunday. Saturday 10–5. Admission by donation. The museum contains 3,000 toys, cars, trucks, lead soldiers, airplanes, boats, dolls, guns, miniature village, a forty-foot diorama of the Charles Dickens' "A Christmas Carol."

Becker Vineyards, 210-644-2681, Hwy. 290 E, 11 miles, right on Jenschke Lane. Open for tours and tastings Monday–Saturday 10–5, Sunday 12–5. Features an antique saloon bar and wood burning fireplace. Vineyard is surrounded by peach orchards and wildflower fields.

Bell Mountain/Oberhellmann Vineyards, 210-685-3297, Highway 16 N (14 miles). Open for tours, tastings and sales Saturday from March through mid December from 10–5, with tours at 11, 1 and 3 and other times by appointment.

Dulcimer Factory & Factory Store, 210-997-6704. 715 S. Washington. Tours Monday–Friday 10:30, 1 on the half hour.

Enchanted Rock State Natural Area, 915-247-3903. RR 965 N (18 miles). Park hours 8 AM–10 PM daily. Admission. Hiking, climbing, backpacking, camping, picnicking, nature study. Enchanted Rock is among the oldest exposed rocks in North America. Group Picnic area with a pavilion.

Fort Martin Scott Historic Site, 210-997-9895, 1606 E. Main, 2 miles east on Hwy. 290. Hours 9–5 Saturday and Sunday year round except Christmas. Admission. Pre-Civil War military post established in 1848 was the first U.S. Army frontier fort in Texas.

The fort was home to at least eight Civil War generals including Confederate James Longstreet. Reconstruction includes the guardhouse, a civilian log cabin and two officers' quarters. Visitor Center includes exhibits about the post including documents and artifacts recovered from the site.

Fredericksburg Brewing Company, 245 E. Main, 210-997-1646. Beers are brewed in the German brewing tradition; located in a restored rock building.

Fredericksburg Herb Farm, 210-997-8615, 402 Whitney Street. Monday–Saturday 9:30–5:30; Sunday 1–4.

Fredericksburg Winery, 210-990-8747 or 990-8566, 247 W. Main. Monday–Thursday 10–6, Friday and Saturday 10–8; Sunday 11–6.

Gish's Old West Museum, 210-997-2794, 502 N. Milam. Come by or call for appointment. Display of Old West relics, including collections of saddles, lawmen's badges and old guns, cowboy attire and an exhibit of western art.

Grape Creek Vineyards, Hwy 290 E (10 miles), 210-644-2710. Open for tour and tastings Monday–Saturday 10–5, Sunday 12–5. Vineyards feature antique roses, bed & breakfast, gift shop, tasting room.

Historic District includes "Sunday Houses," small structures usually with a sleeping loft reached by an outside stairway, erected in town by farmers and ranchers to have a place to stay when they came to buy needed staples, to sell their butter and crops, visit on Saturdays and then attend church on Sundays.

Jeep Collins Jewelry Workshop, 310 Post Oak Road, 210-997-7716 visitor center; 210-997-3135 retail shop. Tours Monday–Friday 9–10:30 and 1:30–3. Lost wax casting method as well as jewelry wrought by hand from silver, brass and gold.

Lady Bird Johnson Municipal Park, 210-997-4202, Texas Hwy. 16 S, 3 miles. Hours 6:30 AM–11 PM (daylight savings) 6:30 AM–10 PM remainder of year. Includes an 18-hole golf course, two putting greens, swimming pool, baseball diamonds, volleyball and tennis courts. Lake for boating (no motors) and fishing. Picnic areas with BBQ grills, outdoor pavilions. Overnight camping areas.

LBJ State and National Historical Parks—Stonewall area, 210-644-2252, Hwy. 290 E, 16 miles. Hours 8–5 daily, except Christmas Day and New Year's Day. Visitor center, park store, Behren's "Dogtrot" Cabin (c. 1840s), outdoor amphitheater, nature trail and Sauer Beckmann Living History Farmstead 8–4:30 daily), depicting traditional German family living in the early 1900s. Exhibits, movie, slide shows, hiking, wildlife displays, picnic and rest areas, playground, dining hall, group picnic area, fishing, swimming, tennis, baseball facilities. Tour buses to see the LBJ Ranch depart from the state park visitor center.

Luckenbach, Texas, 210-997-3224, 5 miles southeast of Fredericksburg off FM 1376, consists of a dancehall, bar and general store. Dances are held monthly.

Pioneer Museum Complex, 210-997-2835, 309 W. Main. Hours Monday–Saturday 10–5; Sunday 1–5. Admission: $3 per person (12 & up). The main museum building, the 1849 stone Kammlah house and store, features eight furnished rooms, a wine cellar, three pioneer kitchens with open hearths, a stone covered hof (yard). Other buildings include the Fassel family limestone home furnished with buggies, a smokehouse, a barn and blacksmith shop, the Walton-Smith log cabin, the authentic Weber Sunday House, the one-room White Oak schoolhouse, and the Fredericksburg Volunteer Fire Department Museum. A home-cooked German meal is offered with a two week notice. Minimum of 15 people. Contact Gillespie County Historical Society, 312 W. San Antonio St., Fredericksburg, TX 78624.

Round Up at Heard Ranch, 210-997-7217 or 824-3328, Tivydale Rd. Show and meal by appointment. A cattle roundup where Heard Ranch cowboys and vaqueros herd, rope, tie and brand calves for visiting spectators. After the demonstration, cowboys answer questions and converse with the guests. Includes a Texas style barbeque from the chuck wagon.

Vereins Kirche Museum, 210-997-2835. Hours Monday–Saturday 10–4, Sunday 1–4. Admission $1.50 per person (12 years and up). Originally constructed in 1847 as a church, meeting hall, school, and fort, this building is the landmark building of Fredericksburg. Vereins Kirche translates to "Society Church." Features pictures and artifacts about life in early Gillespie County. Contact the Gillespie County Historical Society, 312 W. San Antonio St., Fredericksburg, TX 78624.

Wildseed Farms Market Center, 210-990-8080, Hwy 290 E (7 miles). One of the nation's largest working wildflower farms. Market Center includes seeds, wine, peaches, antiques and other Texas Hill Country gifts.

Annual Events: January: Midnight Volksmarch; Gillespie Co. 4-H & FFA Livestock Show; Gem & Mineral Show

February: Masken Ball; Gun & Knife Show; Hug In; Pedernales Promenade

March: St. Francis Xavier Parish Fest; Hereford Association Sale; Mud Dauber Festival & Ball; Country Peddler Show; Nimitz Museum Program; Easter Fires Program

April: Gun & Knife Show; Outdoor Expo; Spring Herb Fest; Spring Real Antiques Show; Pitapat Dance; Wildflower Run & Walk

May: Founder's Day Celebration; Comanche Nation Pow-Wow; Memorial Day Service

June: Artists Invitational Show; Country Peddler Show; Hill Country Golf Classic; June–August Parimutuel Horse Racing; Volkssport Festival; Stonewall Peach JAMboree & Rodeo; Antique Tractor & Engine Show

July: Children's 4th of July Parade; Night in Old Fredericksburg Festival; NIOF Parimutuel Horse Racing; Vor Schuetzenfest; Hill Country Auto Swap Meet & Car Display

August: Bundes Schuetzenfest; Ecumenical Peace Program; Doss Community Fair

October: Oktoberfest; Hill Country Cycle Tour; St. Joseph's Hall Craft Sale; State Chili Championship & Ball; TX Mesquite Art Festival; Nimitz Symposium; Food & Wine Fest

November: Die Kunstler von Fredericksburg Art Show; Veterans Day Salute; Real Antiques Show;

Gun & Knife Show; Regional Christmas Lighting Tour Begins; Country Peddler Show

December: Jaycee Santa Claus Parade; Kinderfest; Pearl Harbor Program; Stonewall Heritage Society Gala; Kristkindl Markt; Candlelight Tour of Homes; Zweiter Weihnachten; New Year's Eve Dance

Accommodations: *Bed & Breakfast/Guesthouse Reservations Services:*

Bed & Breakfast of Fredericksburg, 210-997-4712

Be My Guest, 210-997-7227

Gastehaus Schmidt Reservation Service, 210-997-5612

Hill Country Lodging & Reservation Service, 210-990-8455 or 800-745-3591

Motels:

Best Western Sunday House Inn, 210-997-4484

Budget Host Deluxe Inn, 800-bud-host or 210-997-3344

Comfort Inn, 210-997-9811

Country Inn, 210-997-2185

Days Inn Suites, 800-329-7466

Dietzel Motel, 210-997-3330

Econo Lodge, 219-997-3437

Frederick Motel, 800-996-6050, 210-997-6050

Fredericksburg Inn & Suites, 210-997-0202

Frontier Inn Motel, 210-997-4389

Miller Inn, 210-997-2244

Peach Tree Inn, 800-843-4666, 210-997-2117

Save Inn, 210-997-6568

Stonewall Motel, 210-644-2661

Sunset Motel, 210-997-9581

Restaurants: Alfredo's, 505 W. Main, 210-997-8593

Altdorf Restaurant, 301 W. Main, 210-997-7865

Andy's Diner, 413 S. Washington, 210-997-3744

Auslander Restaurant, 323 E. Main, 210-997-7714

Biggardi's Restaurant, 1035 Hwy. 16 S

China Garden, 116 N. Crockett, 210-997-0231

Church's Chicken, 614 E. Main, 210-997-7333

Circle C Chuckwagon, Hwy. 87 S, 210-997-9893

Cookie Jar, 106 E. Main, 210-997-3499

Dairy Queen, 902 E. Main, 210-997-4648

Der Lindenbaum, 312 E. Main, 210-997-9126

Enchanted Inn, 3 miles N. from Main on RR 965, 210-997-5206

Engel's Deli, 320 E. Main, 210-997-3176

El Gallo Restaurant, 11 Miles out Hwy. 290 W, 210-669-2406

Fredericksburg Brewing Co., 245 E. Main, 210-997-1646

Fredericksburg Herb Farm, 402 Whitney, 210-997-8615

Friedhelm's Bavarian Inn & Bar, 905 W. Main, 210-997-6300

Gallery Restaurant, 230 E. Main, 210-997-8777

George's Old German Bakery, 225 W. Main, 210-997-9084

Golden Corral Restaurant, 518 E. Main, 210-997-6213

Ken Hall Barbecue Place, 1.5 Miles S of Main, Hwy. 87, 210-997-2353

Harry's on the Loop, FM 1323, Willow City Loop, 210-685-3553

Lincoln Street, 111 S. Lincoln, 210-997-8463

Los Compadres Mexican Restaurant, 2 miles from Main, Hwy. 16 N., 210-997-5856

Luckenback Inn, Luckenbach Road, 800-997-1124

Mamacita's Mexican Restaurant & Cantina, 506 E. Main, 210-997-9546

McDonald's, 611 E. Main, 210-997-7600

Navajo Grill, 209 E. Main, 210-990-8289

The Nest, 607 S. Washington, 210-990-8383

Peach Tree Tea Room/The Peach Tree After Hours, 210 S. Adams Street, 800-255-3355, 210-997-9527

Pizza Hut, 1104 E. Main, 210-997-7222

Plateau Cafe, 312 W. Main, 210-997-1853

Porky's Hamburger & Onion Ring Co., 904 W. Main, 210-997-6882

The Queen's Head, 419 W. Main, 210-997-9929

Sonic Drive In, 1106 W. Main, 210-997-7303

Spanish Cellar Bistro, 201 N. Llano, 210-997-9076

Stag's Leap, 755 S. Washington, 210-990-8881

Sunday House Restaurant & Convention Center, 515 E. Main, 210-997-9696

Wheeler's Restaurant, 204 E. Main, 210-990-8180

The White Buffalo, 304 N. Llano, 210-997-9127

Back to Jacksboro

Fort Mason is the last of the forts on the Texas Forts Trail. From here the route travels north through central Texas to Jacksboro and roughly follows the military supply route to Forts Griffin and Richardson. Each of the communities along the way of the supply route benefited from the presence of military traffic as well as from the civilian supply trains traveling along the trail.

From Mason, head northeast along County Road 386 to Fredonia.

Fredonia was settled by W. L. and Samuel P. Hays in the late 1850s. After the Civil War the community began to grow as new settlers moved into the region. In 1879 a post office named Deerton was established, but the name was changed a year later to Fredonia.

117

From Fredonia, head back north- west along State Highway 71 which leads you by Voca in southwest Mc- Culloch County.

The village of Voca was settled in 1879 by John Deans and named for his old home, Voca, Arkansas. Seven miles west of Voca is the site of old Camp San Saba, on the San Saba River.

Camp San Saba was established in 1862 as a station for the Texas Frontier Regiment, and had been used earlier, in 1856, as a camp site for the Texas Rangers who patrolled the region. Ranches and businesses grew up around the camp and became the community of Camp San Saba. The area held its own until the town of Brady emerged and then it dwindled. Some twelve miles west of Camp San Saba on Calf Creek, near FM 1311, is a monument to the feat of James and Rezin P. Bowie, who were beseiged for eight days by Tawakoni Indians until the fierce Bowie brothers fought their way free.

Continue along State Highway 71 to Brady.

Brady, the county seat of McCulloch County, is close to the geographic center of Texas. The county had been created from Bexar County in 1856 and named for Ben McCulloch, a renowned Texas Ranger, Confederate General, and Indian fighter, who was killed at the Battle of Elk Horn in 1862. As early as 1847 John 0. Meusebach, founder of Fredericksburg, met with the Comanche chiefs at Camp San Saba where he paid them $3,000 in presents for their promise to leave his colonists alone. The same year J. J. Gaddings arrived in the area with a survey crew. Among the crew was a young man named Peter Brady who argued that a stream they had encountered was a part of the Concho River. When he was proved to be wrong, the stream was named Brady's Creek. Henry and Nancy Fulcher were the first to settle on Brady Creek during the cattle boom era following the Civil War. Brady City, established on 160 acres of land donated by the Fulchers and Thomas E. Smith, had only a few log houses when it became the county seat in 1876. However, its location on the Dodge City or Western Trail to Kansas gave it a jump start to becoming a thriving community. During World War II a German prisoner-of-war internment camp was located on 360 acres two miles east of Brady. It was one of several such camps scattered across Texas. Its only claim to fame was the fact that Sergeant Joe Gottlief—later known as comedian Joey Bishop—was stationed there.

Running northeast from Brady to **Richland Springs,** *Highway 190 passes through* **Rochelle.**

Rochelle was presumably named for Rochelle, France, though why the founders went so far for a name is not told. Richland Springs, in northwestern San Saba County, was built near springs on Richland Creek and was started as early as 1855 by Jackson J. Brown.

San Saba County was named for the San Saba River which the Spaniards named more than two centuries ago. Like much of the other territory in this region, San Saba is a part of the Fisher-Miller Grant of 3,000,000 acres made by the Republic of Texas. The grant was sold to the *Adelsverein* (Society Noblemen) when John 0. Meusebach was commissioner general of the *Adelsverein.* Muesebach and Robert S. Neighbors, special representative of Governor J. P. Henderson, negotiated a treaty with the Comanches allowing the Germans to settle in the country, but the Germans did not arrive in large numbers in San Saba County. San Saba, settled in 1854, became the county seat when the county was organized in 1856.

An important Indian treaty was made between John H. Rollins, representing the United States, and the Penateka Comanches on Spring Creek—now called Wallace Creek—a few miles west of the site of San Saba. Among the noted chiefs were Buffalo Hump, Yellow Wolf, Ketumseh, White Horse, and Never Stops. The treaty resulted in the release of a number of captives held by the Indians.

From Richland Springs County Road 45 leads north to FM 2126. Go to U. S. Highway 377, which leads to the city of Brownwood.

Brown County was created in 1857 and named for Captain Henry Stephenson Brown, with the city of Brownwood being named the county seat in 1857. In December of 1828, Captain Brown had chased the Comanches into the area near Gonzales, and had recaptured some 500 horses and mules taken by the Indians. A hundred years before, the Spanish under Colonel Don Diego Ortiz Parrilla had also passed through Brown County on their way to the Red River to punish those Indians responsible for the destruction of the San Saba Mission. The arrival of the U. S. Military in the 1850s opened the region for settlement. Between 1852–1854 the old Fort Phantom Hill-Austin road crossed present U. S. Highway 377 about seven miles northeast of Brownwood.

Welcome W. Chandler and his family were the first settlers of Brown County in 1856. During the same year, J. H. Fowler brought the first cattle into the area and John and Anna Williams arrived from Missouri. Williams's Ranch became an important trading center in the southeast corner of the county. Although the ranch was isolated it was never dull and often not serene, according to common reports. Nor was life in the county less exciting. Indians continued to raid the area as late as 1871, and following the Civil War many unsavory characters found their way into and through Brown County.

The 1870s did begin to see changes for the betterment of the region. Brownwood had been originally located on the East side of Pecan Bayou, but in 1875, Judge Greenleaf Fisk donated sixty acres of land to locate the county seat in its present location. Many felt that Greenleaf would fail in his attempt to move the town, but they were wrong. By 1890 land that had seldom sold for more than fifty cents an acre in the 1870s was selling for eight dollars to ten dollars an acre. The arrival of the Santa Fe Railroad on December 1, 1885, secured the new location of Brownwood. Four years later Howard Payne and Daniel Baker Colleges were established in Brownwood, which brought numbers of new residents to the area.

Brownwood's greatest boom period began when the Thirty-Sixth Division (Texas National Guard) and the 111th Air Squadron were ordered to report to the newly created Camp Bowie in September of 1940. With their arrival, Brownwood's population rose from 13,398 in 1940 to 22,479 by March 20, 1941, and yanked the community out of the Depression. Construction jobs abounded both on the base and in town as the city tried to meet the needs of Camp Bowie. Just as Brownwood was adjusting to its new role it had to face the reality that it might lose Camp Bowie when the war began to come to an end. To meet such a possibility a postwar planning committee was created by the Chamber of Commerce and chaired by John Yantis. On August 1, 1946, the War Department declared Camp Bowie "surplus," and offered its facilities for sale. Brownwood was once again faced with a depression, but the people of Brownwood regrouped and built their future on their strengths—agriculture and small industry. (Martin 1967, 31–43)

In 1969 Howard Payne University established the Douglas MacArthur Academy of Freedom, which not only houses a fine museum, but also provides the students of Howard Payne the opportunity to study the problems and challenges facing the nation today.

Take U.S. Highway 377 north to **Comanche.**

Lying northwest of Brown County is Comanche County, started in December, 1854, when five families—Mercer, Collier, Tuggle, Oaks, and Holmsley—pulled off the Fort Phantom Hill road and outspanned their oxen on the south bank of the South Leon River. The county was organized May 17, 1856, at Cora, by one-hundred persons. However,

Cora's days were numbered as the county seat after the county was reduced to create additional counties. T. C. Frost obtained 240 acres along Indian Creek, about fifteen miles northeast of Cora, where T. J. Nabers and Ransom Tuggle laid off the town site of Comanche. The new town, more centrally located, became the county seat in 1859, and Cora was soon no more.

In the late 1850s, Comanche Indians began to assert their claim to the county that bore their name, and in 1861 all residents were concentrated at Comanche, South Leon, and Cora. With their cattle gone and the Indians keeping them from planting crops, the future of the settlers in the region was not promising. However, the arrival of a relief party with supplies from Bell County prevented the abandonment of the settlements.

The end of the Civil War and the westward flow of settlers ended the Indian problem, but Comanche was then plagued with lawlessness—notably the killing of a deputy sheriff by the infamous outlaw John Wesley Hardin. Citizens formed a mob and hanged Joe Hardin, the gunman's brother, along with four of the gunman's friends. John Wesley escaped for the time and later got off with a sentence of twenty-five years in prison. Law and order were soon restored to the community. The arrival of the Fort Worth and Rio Grande Railroad on October 1, 1890, gave a boost to the local economy, which was already shifting from cattle to agriculture. The growth of the town brought the destruction of a grove of oaks that grew where the town square is today. Only the Fleming Oak remains, thanks to Mart Fleming's 10 gauge which convinced the city fathers to let the tree stand. (Lightfoot 1956, 30–43)

Take State Highway 16 north from Comanche to De Leon.

De Leon was established on July 7, 1881, when the Texas Central Railroad decided to build its own town instead of going through Comanche. De Leon's growth was stimulated when the westward progress of the Texas Central was delayed for several years and the city became a terminus town. It was several years before the railroad moved further west thus bringing a lot of business to De Leon. Also the Texas Central Emigration Service brought numerous settlers into the area to be settled on railroad land. De Leon was soon calling itself "The Biggest Little City in the World." In 1896 seventy families from Lafayette County, Mississippi arrived with their livestock and became a part of the growing agricultural community. De Leon soon found its economic growth in peanuts, peaches, and melons.

Desdemona lies on Highway 16 north of De Leon in Eastland County, and was locally known as Hogtown.

Eastland County commemorates the name of William M. Eastland, Texas Ranger and soldier who fell in the Texas Mier Expedition, the last of the raiding expeditions launched from the Republic of Texas into Mexico. The county was organized in 1873, and Eastland became the county seat in 1874.

The area that is Desdemona was settled by C. C. Blair in 1860. His ranch was where people "forted up" during the Civil War when Indians were in the area. In the 1870s the town provided an outlet for the travelers on the Waco-Fort Griffin Road. Originally called Desdemonia, the Post Office Department ordered them to change the name to Desdemona in December of 1901.

The little trading town was transformed overnight when, on September 5, 1918, the workmen on the Joe Duke wildcat well hit oil. The men barely escaped cremation. They were lowering the bit into the well when gas suddenly appeared in great quantity and was ignited by the tool dresser's furnace. The ensuing inferno was heightened by a stream of burning oil that suddenly made its way to the surface and became a column of flame 200 feet high that could be seen in Comanche. The well became a two-thousand-barrel-a-day producer, and began one of the more spectacular booms in oil history. Only a little land in the vicinity was under lease at the time of the discovery, so speculators paid fabulous prices and dotted the townsite with derricks. One lease was recorded for 1/100th of an acre, and one royalty sale for 1/800th of an acre. In 1919 production reached a peak of 7,375,825 barrels then fell sharply because of too rapid production. It was estimated there were 500 wells within a four mile radius of the town.

Desdemona, which had a population of about fifty when oil was discovered, saw thousands of people descend upon their community. The majority of the population were honest and trustworthy, but they were so involved in their efforts to make money that they gave little thought to the environment or the general welfare of the place. Crooks of every sort gathered in the general rush and became parasites on the community. The city officials were unable to cope with the lawless situation, so groups of citizens started banding together for protection and to punish lawbreakers. At times such groups became tyrannical, as on the occasion when they drove every Jew and Greek from the town. Order was finally restored by the Texas Rangers in 1920. Following the oil boom, the community returned to agriculture for its chief source of income, and Desdemona returned to being a small village.

From Desdemona, take FM 2214 west to FM 2461, and then north along the east side of Lake Leon to **Ranger**, *across IH-20.*

Ranger was named for a Texas Ranger camp that had been located nearby. With the arrival of the Texas and Pacific Railroad in October of 1880, the settlers around the community, called Ranger Camp Valley, moved two miles west to the railroad. The town was officially named Ranger in 1883.

Ranger's oil boom began about a year before the one in Desdemona. On October 21, 1917, the McClesky Number 1 well came in as a seventeen-hundred-barrels-per-day producer. The well was completed largely through the energy and persistence of W. K. Gordon of the Texas and Pacific Coal Company, which became the Texas and Pacific Coal and Oil Company. In 1919 Ranger hit its peak as eight producing regions had been opened and the field had produced nearly 4,000,000 barrels of oil. The oil discovery could not have come at a more opportune time. It helped meet the demands of World War I, and oil sold as high as $4.25 a barrel.

Ranger has probably never been surpassed for creating an atmosphere of an exciting race for wealth, with the disarray and confusion that results when a town of a thousand people balloons into a city of thirty thousand within a few months. Flimsy, temporary buildings were crowded. In dry weather the dust was stifling and rain made streets loblollies. At least one enterprising citizen with a horse and sled ferried persons across the street for a fee. Lawlessness and crime were all too prevalent. Texas Rangers aided local officers in law enforcement at times. After a period of time the city swung back into balance. By the mid-1920s, the boom was over and Ranger saw a marked decrease in population. Today it has about 3,000 people and is the home of Ranger Junior College. Its economy is still supported by oil, along with the surrounding agricultural and cattle producers.

*From **Ranger** take IH-20 east to State Highway 16. Go north on State Highway 16 to **Strawn**.*

Strawn was named for Bethel Strawn who settled in the area in 1858. With the arrival of the Texas and Pacific Railroad in 1880, the community found its economic growth based on coal mined to fuel the railroad and heat the homes of West Texas. Thurber, located just southeast of Strawn on IH 20, at one point in its history is supposed to have had 10,000 miners in the coal fields. However, with the shift by the railroads from coal to oil burning locomotives the decline of the area's boom period began. Today its economy is based on agriculture, gas, and oil. Mounds of mine waste may still be seen in the region.

Continue north along State Highway 16 to pass through **Metcalf Gap**. *Where State Highway 16 joins U. S. Highway 180, go east toward* **Palo Pinto** *and* **Mineral Wells**.

Metcalf Gap is an opening in the Palo Pinto Mountains bearing the name of J. J. Metcalf who established his ranch headquarters here in 1856. The pass was used in the 1850s, and during the next decade the road to Fort Griffin passed through the gap to Palo Pinto.

Palo Pinto, first called Golconda, was founded and became the county seat of Palo Pinto County in 1858. One of its early business establishments was an ox treadmill. In the 1860s and 1870s this community had mail and stage service between Weatherford and Fort Griffin. The Palo Pinto *Star* was established by J. C. Son in 1876.

Mineral Wells was begun on the site of a cabin built by Judge J. W. Lynch in 1877. Because of a drouth Judge Lynch dug a well, but the water did not appear to be fit to drink. By 1881 the medicinal qualities of the water had been discovered, and there were enough people in the area to lay out a townsite. The future of the city was assured when in 1885 the Crazy Well, whose waters were said to be able to cure all types of illness, was drilled. Tourists began to arrive to take the waters, and in 1897 the Hexagon House Hotel was constructed to take care of the health seekers. By the 1920s Mineral Wells had four hundred wells and was the Texas health spa to rival Hot Springs, Arkansas. Unfortunately, after World War II the health spa areas began to be replaced by health clubs and by the mid to late sixties the old spa hotels were disappearing from the scene. One of the more prominent ones, the Baker, is being restored by a local group.

Mineral Wells's economy was also altered by the establishment of Camp Wolters in 1925. The camp began when Brigadier General Jacob F. Wolters obtained permission to establish a training camp for the national guard units he commanded. When World War II came along, Mineral Wells leased and purchased land to increase the size of the camp to 7,500 acres where thousands of troops were trained for the war. The military prosperity came to an end when, on June 27, 1946, the War Department ordered Fort Wolters closed. It did have a brief resurgence during the sixties and seventies when it became a training site for helicopter pilots and other troops bound for Vietnam. Fort Wolters today is the site of the F Troop Museum. F Troop along with the Band and Medical Detachment were moved to Mineral Wells in 1923. During its time of service, the Troop has performed service along the Rio Grande from Brownsville to Fort Bliss and during World War II in Burma where it was assigned to clear the enemy from the route of the Burma Road.

Leave Mineral Wells and head north along U. S. Highway 281, which leads to **Jacksboro** *through* **Perrin,** *which grew out of an older settlement started on Keechi Creek in 1854, in spite of the Indian peril which made Keechi Valley rather famous.*

TOURIST INFORMATION

(When possible please call ahead to be sure these services are still available.)

Brady (915/597-3491)

Population:	5,924
Lakes and Parks:	Lake Brady, City Park, Kenneth Medlock Range
Points of interest:	**Heart of Texas Historical Museum** contains early ranch and home exhibits, farm implements, pioneer weapons, vintage photos, and memorabilia. Housed in restored county jail (c. 1910), still exhibiting cells and prisoner hardware. Open Saturday, Sunday, and Monday afternoons. Corner of High and Main Streets, one block west of town square. **McCulloch County Courthouse** **McCulloch County Museum** **Restored Santa Fe Depot** serves as an art gallery and studio, at Depot and North Bridge Streets
Annual events:	January: County Livestock Show and Sale March, June, October: Texas Muzzle Loading Rifle Association May: Cinco de Mayo Celebration, Heart of Texas Golf Tournament June: Miss Heart of Texas Pageant July: Jubilee Celebration, 4th of July, Stan Guffey Memorial Junior Rodeo August: Brady Junior Rodeo September: World Championship Barbecue Goat Cook Off and Arts & Crafts Fair, and Great Goat Gallop, Old Fashioned County Fair
Restaurants:	Catfish Cove, 706 N. Bridge, 915-597-5088

Club Cabe, 506 W. Commerce, 915-597-7522

El Flamingo Restaurant, 1928 S. Bridge, 915-597-0522

Mac's Barbeque, S. Bridge Street, 915-597-2164

Texas Corral, 2346 S. Bridge, 915-597-1722

Brownwood

(915/646-9335)

Chamber of Commerce, P. O. Box 880, Brownwood, TX 76804

Population:	18,641
Lakes:	Lake Brownwood State Recreation Area offers swimming, fishing, boating, hiking, camping, nature study, trailer facilities, rest rooms, shelters, cabins, and group camp accommodations. 23 miles northwest via Texas 279 and Park Road 15. Admission.
Universities:	Howard Payne University and the Douglas MacArthur Academy of Freedom
Points of interest:	**Hall of Christian Civilization** at the Academy displays some of Douglas MacArthur's personal souvenirs. Unique study settings include Mediterranean Room flanked by replicas of Egyptian tomb statues; Magna Carta Hall replica of English castle room; replica of meeting room in Philadelphia's Independence Hall. Tours Monday–Saturday while school is in session. Call 915-646-2502. Austin Avenue (FM 2524) at Coggin Street
	Brown County Museum of History, 200 block of North Broadway near courthouse, contains seven rooms of exhibits in old jail. Open Wednesday 1–4, Saturday 11–4.
	Camp Bowie Memorial Park, honors men of the 36th Infantry Division ("T-Patch"). Features vintage

military equipment, cannon, armor. Located at intersection of Burnett Drive and Travis Road.

Annual events: March: Rattlesnake Round-up and Jaycees Lone Star Fair

July: Brown County Rodeo

September: Pecan Valley Arts Festival, Heart of Texas Shrine Club Circus

Accommodations: Best Western, 401 E. Commerce, 915-646-3511

Gold Key Inn, 515 E. Commerce, 800-646-2551

Post Oak Inn, 800-785-7740

The Troxler House B&B, 915-646-0889

Restaurants: Catfish Heaven, 409 E. Commerce, 915-643-5356

Gomez, 716 W. Commerce, 915-646-9921

The Section Hand Steakhouse, Brady Hwy 377 S, 915-643-1581

Sopalillas, 919 North Bisk, 915-646-9698

Underwood's Cafeteria, 402 W. Commerce, 915-646-6110

Specialty Shopping: Antique Mall, 114 Early Blvd., 915-643-5562

Mary's Antiques, 1101 Early Blvd., 915-646-9503

Comanche

(915/356-3233)

Chamber of Commerce, 100 Indian Creek Drive, Comanche, TX 76442

Population: 4,343

Lakes and recreation: Lake Proctor, fishing, boating, swimming, and golf

Points of interest: **Comanche County Historical Museum** contains covered wagon, surrey, Indian and pioneer artifacts housed in replica of frontier store.

Fleming Oak, only remaining member of a large grove of oaks which legend says was saved from destruction by an ancient settler who said the tree saved his life during an Indian attack and he would protect the tree with his life.

Old Cora, the oldest existing Texas courthouse

City Park, swimming and Twin Creek hiking Trail

Annual Events: January: Comanche County Junior Livestock Show

April, June, October, November and December: "Old Cora" Trade Days

July: 4th Celebration; Annual Rodeo and Dance on the third weekend of the month

September: Comanche County Pow-Wow, cook-off, entertainment, arts and crafts, classic car show, antique tractor and farm equipment show

December: Lights of Christmas Parade

Accommodations: American Motel, 1301 E. Central, 915-356-2508

Comanche Motor Inn, 508 W. Central, 915-356-2543

Poor Boy Motel, 706 E. Central, 915-356-2808

The Guest House at Heritage Hill B&B, 915-356-3397

It's About Time B&B, 915-356-3345

Rattlesnake B&B, 915-356-7098

Restaurants: The Golden Arrow Cafe, 901 W. Central, 915-356-3217

Jordon's, 500 W. Central, 915-356-3336

Miguels Little Mexico, 1000 E. Central, 915-356-5368

Crow's Nest Cafe, 113 W. Grand, 915-356-3360

Starbeau's, 134 W. Central, 915-356-2869

The Bar-B-Q Shed, 404 E. Central, 915-356-2869

Specialty Shopping:

Bolt's, 406 E. Central, 915-356-7070
Casteberry's Creations, 201 W. Grand, 915-356-3901
Comanche Trading Post, 300 W. Central
The Red Store Mall, 113 W. Grand, 915-356-3360
Red Top, 605 W. Central, 915-356-3173
Selections on the Square, 127 N. Houston, 915-356-3153
This Old House, 700 W. Central, 915-356-2241

De Leon (254/893-2083)

Population:	2,292
Lakes:	Lake Leon and Lake Proctor
Annual events:	August: Peach and Melon Festival
Accommodations:	De Leon Motor Inn, Hwy 6 W, 254-893-2037
Restaurants:	Aunt Annie's Kitchen, 605 N. Fannin, 254-893-4176
	Cisneroz Cafe, 100 N. Houston, 254-893-5181
	Dairy Queen, 600 N. Fannin, 254-893-6804
	Garza's Mexican Restaurant, 408 N. Fannin, 254-893-6263
	La Don's, 410 W. Navarro, 254-893-2100
	La Ressie's Kitchen, 254-893-6675
	Mi Casa Es Su Casa, 408 N. Fannin, 254-893-6263
	Mozell's Country Kitchen, Hwy 6 W, 254-893-2521
	Pizza Pro, 104 W. Navarro, 254-893-4119
	Rollie's on Texas, 307 S. Texas, 254-893-2591
Specialty Shopping:	DeLeon Restoration Works, 103 N. Texas, 254-893-3862

Mineral Wells

(940/325-2557)

Chamber of Commerce, 511 E. Hubbard, 800-252-MWTX or 940-325-2557

Population:	15,256
Lakes and Parks:	Lake Mineral Wells State Park, Possum Kingdom Lake, Lake Palo Pinto, West City Park, Donald Burns Memorial Rose Garden at Woodland Park Cemetery, Pollard Creek Park,
Points of interest:	**Baker Hotel** **Bat World** **Boudreau Gardens Herb Farm** **Crazy Water Hotel** **Famous Water Company**, founded in 1913 by Edward P. Dismuke, is the only mineral water well in operation today. The drinking pavilion, well, and bottling plant are at 209 N.W. 6th. Open Monday, Wednesday, Friday 9–5, Saturday 9–12. **Historic Downtown** **Little Rock Schoolhouse** **Old Jailhouse Museum** (Palo Pinto) **Santa's Forest**
Annual events:	February: Crazy Chili Cook-Off March: Palo Pinto County Livestock Show and Fair; Gospel Convention; Mineral Wells Antique Automotive Swap Meet April: All-Star Basketball Classic; National Stock Dog Futurity May: Palo Pinto County Livestock Association Rodeo July: Fireworks at Holiday Hills Country Club; Fireworks at Possum Kingdom Lake

August–September: Southern Airways Reunion; Best Little Balloonfest in Texas, Possum Kingdom

October: Crazy Water Festival; The Great Outdoors Barbecue Cook-Off, Possum Kingdom

November: Veteran's Day Celebration; Christmas Tree Lighting

December: Crystal Christmas; Festival of Lights on Possum Kingdom Lake; Christmas Parade; Zonta Holiday Home Tour

Accommodations: Budget Host Inn, 3601 E. Hubbard 800-Bud-Host, 940-325-3377

HoJo Inn, 2809 Hwy 180 W, 800-I-Go-Ho-Jo, 940-328-1111

Ramada Limited, 4103 Hwy 180 E, 800-2Ramada, 940-325-6956

Silk Stocking Row Bed & Breakfast, 415 N.W. 4th, 940-325-4101

Skyline Motel, 3603 E. Hubbard, 940-325-4433

Victorian House Bed & Breakfast, Weatherford, TX, 800-687-1660, 940-596-8295, 599-9600

Restaurants: Braum's Ice Cream & Dairy Stores, 3201 N.E. 2nd, 940-328-1672

The Cafe, Baker Hotel, 207 E. Hubbard, 940-325-8600

Chicken Express, 213 N.E. 27th, 940-325-6909

Dairy Mart, 700 S.E. 1st, 940-325-6983

Dairy Queen of Mineral Wells, 2300 E. Hubbard, 940-325-5311

Days Cafe, 3701 Hwy 180 E, 940-325-6208

The Green Onion, 1396 S. FM 4, 940-769-3208

Holiday Hills Country Club, Hwy 180 E, 940-325-9442

K-Bob's Steakhouse, 1701 E. Hubbard, 940-325-0171

Lake Palo Pinto Marina & Restaurant, Palo Pinto, TX, 940-769-2911

McDonald's Restaurant, 100 Garrett Morris Parkway, 940-325-7307

Palace Tearoom, 113 N. Oak, 940-325-9508

Pulido's Mexicsan Restaurant, 100 N. E. 22nd, 940-325-8664

Shotgun's Bar-B-Que, 215 N. E. 27th, 940-325-4242

Taco Bell, 2103 E. Hubbard, 940-325-0641

Woody's Tavern, 6105 Hwy 180 E, 940-325-9817

Specialty Shopping:

Anita's Antiques & Collectibles, 307 N. Oak, 940-325-1455

Colonial Accents, 2401 N. Oak, 940-325-3866

Richey's Antiques and Uniques, 1201 E. Hubbard, 940-325-5940

Sarah Jane's Antiques, Crafts & Collectibles, 115 N. Oak, 940-325-3005

Texas Hummingbird, 800-A E. Hubbard, 940-328-1880

Two for Country Gifts & Gallery, 109 N. Oak, 940-328-0022

VF Outlet Mall 4500 Hwy 180 E, 940-325-3318

Wild Rose Antiques, Collectibles & Crafts, 213 N. Oak, 940-325-2337

Wynnewood Antique Mall, 2502 Hwy 180 E, 940-325-9791

Ranger
(254/647-3091)

Population:	2,822
Colleges:	Ranger Junior College
Points of interest:	**Roaring Ranger Museum** contains artifacts and photos of the city's oil boom days, housed in the old depot. Also houses Chamber of Commerce office, Commerce and Main streets downtown **J. H. McCleskey #1**, site of 1,700 barrel-per-day oil gusher that touched off Ranger's oil boom in 1917.
Annual Events:	May: Spring Fly-In by EAA Chapter #956 June: Annual Old Time Country Festival July: July 4th Annual Rodeo September: Roaring Ranger Day (Last Saturday) October: Annual EAA Chapter #956 Fly-In; Chili-Barbeque Cookoff; Remembering Historical McCleskey No. 1. December: Annual Christmas Tree Lighting and Parade

Additional Forts

Additional forts in Texas that are not on the designated Texas Forts Trail but that will be of interest:

FORT BLISS

Fort Bliss, located in El Paso, is a U. S. Army post established in 1848 as defense against hostile Indians and to assert U. S. authority over lands acquired after the Mexican War. Headquarters for Confederate forces in the Southwest during the Civil War, it was later a refitting post for military efforts against Apache chief Geronimo. Today it is used as a U. S. Army Air Defense Center and for combat training for allied nations.

Fort Bliss Replica Museum is located at Pleasanton Road and Sheridan Drive, Building 600. The museum has a replica of the adobe buildings of Fort Bliss. A walk through the buildings takes you on a history tour of the fort from 1848 to 1948. Open daily 9–

4:30. Closed Christmas, New Year's, Easter and Thanksgiving. For additional information call 915-568-4518.

El Paso

Population:	583,431
Altitude:	3,762
Points of Interest:	**El Paso Convention and Visitors Bureau**, 1 Civic Center Plaza

Border Patrol Museum, 4315 Transmountain Road (Loop 375), Tuesday–Sunday 9–5.

Chamizal National Memorial, Paisano and San Marcial Streets, daily 8–5.

Concordia Cemetery, Exit I-10 at Copia, historic cemetery and landmark, includes grave of gunfighter John Wesley Hardin

El Paso Centennial Museum, University of Texas at El Paso, University Avenue and Wiggins Road, Tuesday–Friday 10–3; Sunday 1:30–5:30

El Paso Holocaust Museum and Study Center, 401 Wallenberg, 915-833-5656. Open Sunday–Thursday 1–4.

El Paso Museum of Art, 1211 Montana Avenue, Tuesday–Saturday 10–5; Sunday 1–5.

El Paso Museum of History, I-10 at Loop 375 (Avenue of the Americas), Tuesday–Sunday 9–4:45.

Air Defense Artillery Museum, Fort Bliss, Building 5000, Pleasanton Road near Robert E. Lee Road, daily 9–4:30. Closed Christmas, New Year's, Easter and Thanksgiving.

Museum of the Noncommissioned Officer, Biggs Army Airfield, Building 11331, Barksdale & 5th

Streets, Monday–Friday 9–4; Saturday, Sunday 12–4.

Franklin Mountain State Park, Woodrow Bean and Transmountain Road. 915-566-6441

Hueco Tanks State Park, off US Highway 62/180, 26 miles east of El Paso. Admission.

Magoffin Home State Historic structure, 1120 Magoffin, 9–4 daily. Admission.

Old Missions:

Nuestra Senora del Carmen, 100 block of Old Pueblo Road (Zaragosa exit from I-10 east)

Nuestra Senora de la Concepcion del Socorro, present village of Socorro adjacent to southeast El Paso, FM 258 south.

San Elizario Presidio Chapel, FM 258 south.

Tigua Indian Reservation: Ysleta del Sur Pueblo, 915-859-7913; 305 Yaya Lane (off Socorro Rd). Open Tuesday–Friday 9–4; Saturday, Sunday 9–5.

FORT CLARK

Fort Clark, located on US Hwy 90 on the east side of Brackettville, was established on June 20, 1852, at Las Moras Spring in Kinney County by companies C and E of the First Infantry under the command of Major Joseph H. LaMotte. Its basic purpose was to guard the border, protect the military road to El Paso, and deal with the Indian problems of the region. Notable military officers who served here include Colonel Ranald S. Mackenzie, Generals George C Patton and George C. Marshall. The fort was deactivated in 1944, and served in various capacities until it was purchased by the North American Towns of Texas and turned into a private recreation and retirement community. Today many of the old quarters with names such as Mackenzie, Shafter, Bullis,

Bliss, Wainright, and Patton can be slept in by visitors to the site. Old Guardhouse Museum has local and pioneer history exhibits. Saturday, Sunday 1–4. For information about the park call 830-563-2493, 800-937-1590.

Brackettville

Population:	1,883
Altitude:	1,110
Points of Interest:	**Alamo Village**, 7 miles north on RM 674, is a recreation center built around the movie set for John Wayne's *The Alamo*, filmed in 1959. One of the largest and most complete sets ever constructed in the U.S., the Alamo replica was built by adobe craftsmen from Mexico. It overlooks a complete frontier village of the 1800s. Operated by Shahan Angus Ranch, the set includes a cantina-restaurant, trading post, Indian store, authentic stage depot, old-time jail, bank, saddle shop, and other typical Old West structures. During the summer months visitors see shows, often interrupted by shoot-outs between frontier lawmen and desperados. Open daily at 9 AM. Admission.

Historic Buildings: St. Mary Magadalene Catholic Church dates from 1878; Masonic Lodge Building c. 1879, was the original county courthouse.

Seminole Indian Scout Cemetery, 3 miles south on county road, dates from the frontier era. The scouts were descended from slaves stolen from plantations by Florida Seminoles. Moved to Oklahoma after the Seminole War, many scouts migrated toward Mexico. The Army hired 150 as scouts to follow trails

of raiding Indians. A group settled in Brackettville around Fort Clark. Descendants remain as farmers and ranchers and maintain the old cemetery which includes the graves of four Medal of Honor winners.

FORT DAVIS

In October of 1854, Brevet General Persifor F. Smith, commanding the Department of Texas, selected the site of Fort Davis and named the post after Secretary of War Jefferson Davis. Six companies of the Eighth United States Infantry under Lieutenant Colonel Washington Seawell arrived at Painted Comanche Camp, the site of an Indian village, on Limpia Creek to build and garrison the post. Confederate cavalry under Colonel John R. Baylor occupied the fort for almost a year, then retreated to San Antonio after failing to take New Mexico.

Federal troops under Lieutenant Colonel Wesley Merritt reoccupied the fort and began construction of a new post. Fort Davis became a major installation with quarters for more than 600 men and more than sixty adobe and stone structures. From 1867 to 1885 the post was garrisoned primarily by units composed of white officers and black "buffalo soldiers," enlisted men of the Ninth and Tenth United States Cavalry regiments and the Twenty-fourth and Twenty-fifth United States Infantry regiments, who compiled a notable record of military achievements against the Apaches and Comanches.

In 1879 Apache chief Victorio and Mescalero Apache warriors began a series of attacks in the area west of Fort Davis. Colonel Benjamin H. Grierson led troops from Fort Davis and other posts against the raiders. After several hard-fought engagements, Victorio retreated to Mexico where he and many of his followers were killed in a battle with Mexican troops. The military usefulness of Fort Davis was over and the fort was ordered abandoned in 1891. (*The New Handbook of Texas*, 1096-97)

Fort Davis

Chamber of Commerce, 915-426-3015

Fort Davis National Historic Site, P. O. Box 1456, State Highways 17-118, Fort Davis, TX 79734. 915-426-3224. FAX 915-426-3122. Open Daily in the summer 8–6; winter 8–5. Closed Christmas Day. The site can be reached from I-10 on the north, and US 90 on the south, by Texas 17 and 118, and from US 90 on the west, Texas 505, 166 and 17. The town of Marfa is 21 miles to the south. Admission.

Population:	900
Altitude:	5,050
Points of Interest:	**Fort Davis National Historic Site**, located on the north edge of the town of Fort Davis, on State Highways 17 and 118, is an excellently preserved fort. Operated by the National Park Service, Fort Davis is an excellent example of frontier forts, including both ruins and restorations. Five restored and refurnished buildings are open on a self-guided basis. Interpreters, dressed in period costumes, are stationed at some of these buildings during the summer months. A museum, open daily in reconstructed barracks, interprets frontier military life, including a sound re-creation of a nineteenth-century military parade—bugles and hoofbeats, the clank and jangle of mounted troops, music from band manuals of 1875, echoing over the empty parade ground. Admission.
	The town of Fort Davis, county seat of Jeff Davis County, established when the fort was built by the

U. S. Army in 1854, retains many remnants of its past. Fort Davis has the longest unpaved stretch (over one mile) of the San Antonio-El Paso Road still in use, with original adobe structures along its route. These buildings, many dating back to the 1870s are part of a self-guided driving tour. Other restored historic structures are sprinkled through town. The Methodist Church was built in 1884; every building on Fort Davis' square, except the post office, dates to the early 1900s. The courthouse and the four-celled jail, now used as the public library, were also built during this period.

Adobe Hacienda Gallery, located one mile on cemetery road, has bronzes, oil, watercolor and leather pictures; books; western and military subjects.

Art Gallery of Western paintings, sculptures, books on the main street

The Art Gallery-Elsie Voigt, 17 miles from Fort Davis on Hwy. 166; 500 sketches in charcoal, water color, tempra and oil, railroad, landscape, and animal art.

Chihuahuan Desert Visitor Center, botanic gardens and nature trails related to the desert flora. On Texas 118, 3.5 miles south. Open May–August, Monday–Friday, 1–5; Saturday, Sunday 9–5.

Jeff Davis County Court House includes an arboretum of trees native to the county.

Davis Mountains State Park, in a sloping basin among the Davis Mountains, 2,869 acres with the primary service facility a multilevel hotel called the Indian Lodge, patterned in the pueblo style. Area interpretive center is open afternoons, June through August, featuring plant and animal material, both live and mounted; bird observation window and wildlife watering station. Camping, picnicking, dining room, trailer facilities, rest rooms, nature study, hiking. Six miles west of Fort Davis, Texas, 118 Park Road 3. Admission.

Limpia Hotel, restored country inn, (c. 1912), turn-of-the-century oak furniture, second story verandah and glassed-in sunporch; Boarding House restaurant. Two other restored buildings, plus cottage. Hotel Limpia Dining Rooms include the Sutter's Club. On the town square. 915-426-3237, 800-662-5517.

Neill Museum contains antique toys made in Texas, including antique dolls, bottles, and furniture. In historic 1898 Truehart House, seven blocks west of the courthouse. Open all year. 915-426-3969 and 426-3838.

Overland Trail Museum, named for the historic trail that once passed its front door, the small museum was the former home, office and shop of Nick Mersfelter, early resident who was the justice of the peace, barber, and area music master. Austrian-born Mersfelter, who could play almost any instrument, was once member of the San Antonio Philharmonic Orchestra. Contains pioneer ranch, trail, and law enforcement artifacts. Open Wednesday–Sunday afternoons in summer. Admission.

Prude Guest Ranch, six miles west on Texas 118, was established in 1889 as a cattle ranch. The ranch is popular for meetings and vacations. Horseback riding, hay rides, chuck wagon cookout, and more. For information/reservations, call 800-458-6232.

University of Texas McDonald Observatory at Mount Locke, 16 miles northwest, via Texas 118,

Spur 78, was built in 1932 following a bequest from William J. McDonald. Located on 6,791 foot peak of Mount Locke, the site was selected because of clear air, high ratio of cloudless nights, distance from a concentration of artificial lights, and dust and radiation filtering growths of shrubs and timber. A visitor center at the foot of Mount Locke presents programs daily 9–5. Each Tuesday, Friday and Saturday evening, weather permitting, the center conducts "Star Parties" for the general public, with viewing of stars and planets through telescopes set up by the observatory. Once a month, visitors can view celestial objects through 107-inch telescope. A fee is charged for the large telescope viewing. Reservations, 915-426-3640.

Special Events: Friends of Fort Davis Festival, the Saturday of Labor Day weekend; special evening tours in the Fall and Spring; various interpretive programs throughout the year. For up-to-date information call 915-426-3224

Accommodations: Boynton House Bed & Breakfast, Guest Lodge, Mexican colonial hacienda atop Dolores Mt., 1/2 miles S. of TDOT, 915-426-3123, 800-358-5929

The Carriage House, Woodward and 4th Streets, 3 blocks west of the courthouse. 915-426-3311, 426-3483

Crow's Nest, west of Fort Davis on Hwy 166, 915-426-3300

Davis Mountains Community Headquarters, west of Fort Davis off Hwy. 166. 915-426-3872, 426-3918

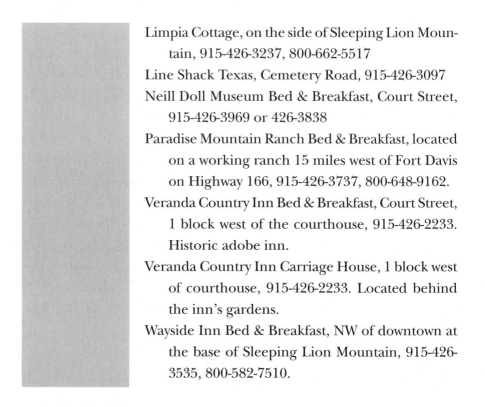

Limpia Cottage, on the side of Sleeping Lion Mountain, 915-426-3237, 800-662-5517

Line Shack Texas, Cemetery Road, 915-426-3097

Neill Doll Museum Bed & Breakfast, Court Street, 915-426-3969 or 426-3838

Paradise Mountain Ranch Bed & Breakfast, located on a working ranch 15 miles west of Fort Davis on Highway 166, 915-426-3737, 800-648-9162.

Veranda Country Inn Bed & Breakfast, Court Street, 1 block west of the courthouse, 915-426-2233. Historic adobe inn.

Veranda Country Inn Carriage House, 1 block west of courthouse, 915-426-2233. Located behind the inn's gardens.

Wayside Inn Bed & Breakfast, NW of downtown at the base of Sleeping Lion Mountain, 915-426-3535, 800-582-7510.

FORT DUNCAN

Fort Duncan, located on the east side of the Rio Grande just above Eagle Pass, was established on March 27, 1849, by Captain Sidney Burank, and occupied by three companies of the First U. S. Infantry Regiment. During the Civil War the post was occupied by Confederate troops of the Frontier Regiment. Federal troops reoccupied the post in 1868. It remained under military authority until 1916. Its primary purpose was to protect the trade crossing into Mexico and travelers along the road to El Paso. It was taken over by the city in 1935, and today many restored stone buildings form the center of a municipal park and country club. The old headquarters serves as a museum. For additional information call 830-773-1714 or 773-2748.

Eagle Pass

Population:	24,806
Altitude:	797
Points of Interest:	**International bridge to Piedras Negras**, across the Rio Grande in Mexico, connects US 57 with Mexico 57 that leads to Monclova, Saltillo, San Luis Potosi and Mexico City. Piedras Negras has many shops with handicraft items and a traditional Mexican market area; restaurants and popular night clubs; bullfights at intervals throughout summer months. **Kickapoo Indian federal reservation**, eight miles south of the city, is being developed. **Lucky Eagle Casino**, off FM 1021 at Rosita Valley Road, operated by the Kickapoo Indians, features a bingo hall and state-of-the-art equipment for gambling. Call 830-758-1936.

FORT LANCASTER

Fort Lancaster is located on old US Hwy 290 ten miles east of Sheffield and thirty-three miles west of Ozona in Crockett County. It was established as Camp Lancaster on August 20, 1855, by Captain Stephen D. Carpenter. The large rectangle around the parade ground was the site of twenty-five buildings that housed two companies of the First U. S. Infantry. Troopers on mules protected wagon trains on the San Antonio-El Paso "lower road." The fort was abandoned in 1861. In the 1970s, excavation of the site produced numerous artifacts which are on display at the visitors center at the Fort Lancaster State Historic Site. 915-836-4391.

Ozona

Population:	3,335
Altitude:	2,348
Points of Interest:	**Crockett County Memorial Fair Park**, east edge of city off US 290, is the present location of Emerald House, the oldest dwelling in the county. The house was moved from the town of Emerald when Ozona became county seat in 1891.
	Crockett County Museum, 404 11th, contains frontier antiques, Indian relics, artifacts from Fort Lancaster, ranch implements and household items of the Western frontier. Open Monday–Friday 10–6.
	David Crockett Monument, statue in city park on the town square, honors the legendary frontiersman and hero of the Alamo for whom the county was named.

FORT LEATON

Fort Leaton State Historic Site is located on Farm Road 170 three miles east of Presidio on a bluff overlooking the Rio Grande. The massive adobe fortress was built by frontiersman Ben Leaton immediately after the Mexican War at this strategic site on the Chihuahua-San Antonio Trail. Leaton cornered lucrative trade with area Indians, supplied far-ranging U. S. Army patrols, and was accused of encouraging Indian raids on settlements in Mexico by trading weapons and ammunition for stolen livestock. Of more than forty original rooms around the large patio, twenty-four are architecturally restored and roofed with cottonwood vigas and rajas, sheathed with adobe. Restoration eventually will include frontier furnishings of living and guest quarters, dining room, kitchen, storerooms, and granary. Interpretive exhibits trace area history and culture; audiovisual program on desert ecology. The area around Fort Leaton has been continuously occupied since 1500 BC. Open daily 8–4:30. Closed December 25. Admission. 915-229-3613.

Presidio

Population:	3,544
Altitude:	2,594
Points of Interest:	**Visitor center at the fort** introduces the Big Bend Ranch State Natural Area and is the departure point for Texas Parks and Wildlife Department bus tours the first Saturday of each month. Tours include a chuck wagon lunch. Tour fee; reservations advisable, 915-229-3613.
	El Camino del Rio, "The River Road," is the local name for FM 170 that stretches from Lajitas northwest to Presidio and beyond into the Chinati Mountains.

Lajitas

Population:	48
Altitude:	2,440
Points of Interest:	Recent developments feature a modern **motel and resort complex** with golf course, river rafting, swimming pools, tennis courts, horseback riding, restaurant, and frontier building styles with plank sidewalks and hitching rails. 915-424-3471.
	Big Bend Ranch State Natural Area, hiking and backpacking, nature study, river rafting and canoeing, bus tours. Entrance and use fees. Warnock

Environmental Education Center, archeological, historical and natural history profile of the Big Bend region. Departure point for the tours of the Big Bend Ranch State Natural Area the third Saturday of each month. Tour fee includes meal in the natural area; reservations advisable. 915-424-3327. Open 8–5 daily. Admission.

FORT STOCKTON

Fort Stockton, constructed of adobe and named for Robert Field Stockton, was established by the United States Army on March 23, 1859, at Comanche Springs, which was within the site of the present city of Fort Stockton, for the protection of the mail service, travelers, and freighters. Comanche Springs was a favorite stop on the Comanche Trail to Chihuahua, the Old San Antonio Road, the Butterfield Overland Mail route, and the San Antonio-Chihuahua freight-wagon road. Captain Arthur T. Lee, commanding Company C, Eighth Infantry, abandoned the post in April 1861. The post was reoccupied by Captain Charles L. Pyron, in command of Company B. Second Regiment, Texas Mounted Rifles, until it was abandoned by the Confederates after General Henry H. Sibley's defeat in New Mexico.

After the Civil War the fort was reoccupied by General Edward Hatch, who made it the headquarters for the Ninth United States Cavalry, a regiment of black troops who were used for patrols, escorts, and scouts, largely against the Apaches. After the defeat of the Apaches the army began withdrawing troops. Since their abandonment by the military, some of the officers' quarters have been used continuously for residences.

Fort Stockton

Population: 9,072

Points of Interest: **Fort Stockton** is located in Fort Stockton, on Hwy 290/67 on the way from San Antonio to El Paso. It contains three officers' quarters; a guard house with jailers' quarters, holding cell and solitary confinement; two enlisted men's barracks and their accompanying kitchens have been reconstructed. Open Monday–Saturday, 10–1 and 2–5. Admission. 300 E. 3rd. 915-336-2400

Annie Riggs Hotel Museum, 301 S. Main, built in 1899, a popular stop on the stage route. Restored and maintained by the local historical society. Fourteen rooms display area collections: 19th-century clothing, photography, Indian artifacts, cowboy regalia, kitchen utensils, geology, religion, Camp Stockton artifacts. Open daily Monday–Saturday 10–12 and 1–5; Sunday 1:30–5. Admission. 915-336-2167

Courthouse Square historic features include the 1883 courthouse, first Catholic Church (1875); first schoolhouse (1883); Zero Stone placed by a survey party in 1859, used as origin point for all land surveys in this part of West Texas. Nearby St. Stephens Episcopal Church (1872).

Grey Mule Saloon, a restored old saloon, was one of early-day "red-eye" dispensaries of West Texas. Callaghan and Main streets.

Historical Sites tour, special signs provide guidance for a tour of historic sites. Historical notations date from days of Cabeza de Vaca's explorations in 1534, and other explorers such as Espejo in 1583, and Mendosa in 1684.

James Rooney County Park, on southern edge of the city at historic Comanche Springs. Swimming, picnicking and tennis courts.

Old Fort Cemetery, records on existing tombstones indicate few people lived beyond age forty.

Paisano Pete, at twenty feet long and eleven feet tall, is probably the world's largest roadrunner. US 290 at Main street.

Tunis Creek Stagecoach Stop, former way station on Butterfield Overland Mail Route; later a Texas Ranger station. Historic structure was moved to a highway rest area on US 290, twenty miles east. Original location was approximately two miles south.

Visitor Information Center has information on dining, accommodations, events, other area information, I-10 and US 285. For information, call 915-336-8052; 800-336-2166.

Accommodations:

Atrium the Inn, 1801 W. Dickinson, 915-336-2274

Atrium the Inn, 1305 NW US Hwy 285, 915-336-6666

Best Values Inn, 901 E. Dickinson, 915-336-2251

Best Western Sunday House Inn, 3201 W. Dickinson, 915-336-8521

Budget Inn, 801 E. Dickinson, 915-336-3311

Comanche Motel and Mobile Home Park, 1301 E. Dickinson, 915-336-5824

Days Inn, 1408 NW US Highway 285, 915-336-7500

Deluxe Inn, 500 E. Dickinson, 915-336-2231

Econo Lodge Business Hwy 290, 800 E. Dickinson, 915-336-9711

Gateway Lodge, 501 E. Dickinson, 915-336-8336

Restaurants:

Adams Pit Shop, Pecos Hwy, 915-336-8776

Alfredo's Mexican Restaurant, 2103 W. Dickinson, 915-336-7116

Best Western Swiss Clock Inn, 3201 W. Dickinson, 915-336-8521

Bienvenidos, 405 W. Dickinson, 915-336-3615

Burrito Express, 100 E. 18th, 915-336-9162

Burrito Inn, 805 N. Alamo, 915-336-3141

Courtyard Restaurant, 800 E. Dickinson, 915-336-9711

Dairy Queen, 408 W. Dickinson, 915-336-5660

El Corral Restaurant, 2601 W. IH-10, 915-336-5578

Gulf's Best Seafood House, Inc., 2003 W. Dickinson, 915-336-9977

BIBLIOGRAPHY

Bierschwale, Margaret. Fort Mason, Texas. Mason, Texas: n.p., 1968.

Bitner, Grace. "Early History of the Concho Country and Tom Green County." *West Texas Historical Association Year Book*. Vol. IX. October, 1933.

Conger, Roger N. "Fort Concho." *Frontier Forts of Texas*. Waco, Texas: Texian Press, 1966.

Cummins, M. L., editor. "Colonel J. K. F. Mansfield's Report of the Inspection of the Department of Texas in 1856." *Southwestern Historical Quarterly*. Vol. XLII, April 1939.

_____. "Notes and Documents, W. G. Freeman's report on the Eighth Military Department." *Southwestern Historical Quarterly*. Vol. LIII, October 1949; January 1950; April 1950.

Downs, Fane, editor *The Future Great City of West Texas, Abilene: 1881–1891.* Abilene: n.p. 1981.

Dodge, Richard Irving. *Our Wild Indians: Thirty-Three Year's Personal Experience Among the Red Men of the Great West.* Hartford, Connecticut: A. D. Worthington and Co., 1883.

Fort Concho: National Historical Landmark, San Angelo, Texas: A Masterplan for Development. Austin: Bell, Mein and Hoffman Architects and Restoration Consultants, Inc., 1980.

Pierce, N. H. *The Free State of Menard: A History of the County.* Menard, Texas: Menard News Press, 1946.

Gregory, J. N. "Fort Concho, Its Why and Wherefore." *Newsfoto Yearbooks*. San Angelo, Texas, 1957.

Haley, J. Evetts. "Fort Concho and the Texas Frontier." San Angelo, Texas: *San Angelo Standard Times*, 1952.

Hamilton, Allen Ike. *Sentinel of the Southern Plains: Fort Richardson and the Northwest Texas Frontier, 1866–1878.* Fort Worth: Texas Christian University, 1988.

Huckabay, Ida Lasater. *Ninety-Four Years in Jack County, 1854–1948.* Jacksboro: n.p. 1949.

Ledbetter, Barbara A. Neal. *Fort Belknap: A Frontier Saga.* Burnet, Texas: Eakin Press, 1982.

Lightfoot, B. B. "From Frontier to Farmland: Highlights of the History of Comanche Country." *West Texas Historical Association Year Book*. Vol. XXXII. October, 1956.

Martin, Tessica. "Brownwood, Texas and World War II." *West Texas Historical Association Year Book.* Vol. LII. October, 1967.

Richardson, Rupert N. *The Frontier of Northwest Texas, 1846 to 1876.* Glendale, California: Arthur H. Clark Company, 1963.

_____ and Carl Coke Rister. *The Greater Southwest.* Glendale, California: Arthur H. Clark Company. 1934.

Rister, Carl Coke. "The Border Post of Phantom Hill." *West Texas Historical Association Year Book.* Vol. XIV. October, 1938.

_____. *Fort Griffin on the Texas Frontier.* Norman, Oklahoma: Oklahoma Press, 1956.

_____. *The Southwestern Frontier, 1865–1881.* Cleveland, Ohio: Clark Co., 1928.

Simpson, Harold. "Fort Mason." *Frontier Forts of Texas.* Waco, Texas: Texian Press, 1966. •

Sullivan, Jerry M. "Fort McKavett, 1852–1883." *West Texas Historical Association Year Book.* Vol. XLV, 1969.

Wallace, Ernest. "Ranald S. Mackenzie on the Texas Frontier." *The Museum Journal.* Volume VII–VIII. F. E. Green, editor. Lubbock, Texas: West Texas Museum Association, Texas Technological College, 1963–1964.

War Department, Surgeon General's Office. *A Report on the Hygiene of the United States Army, with Descriptions of Military Posts.* Circular Number 8. Washington, D. C.: Government Printing Office, 1875.

Whisenhunt, Donald K. "Fort Richardson." *West Texas Historical Association Year Book.* Vol. XXXIX. October, 1963.

INDEX

B. W. Aston is chairman of the History Department and director of the Rupert N. Richardson Research Center at Hardin-Simmons University.

Donathan Taylor is assistant professor of history at Hardin-Simmons University in Abilene, Texas.